I0079553

LESLIE BUSWELL

AMBULANCE NUMBER 10

AMBULANCE NO. 10

PERSONAL LETTERS FROM
THE FRONT

BY

LESLIE BUSWELL

The Naval & Military Press Ltd

Published by

The Naval & Military Press Ltd
Unit 10 Ridgewood Industrial Park,
Uckfield, East Sussex,
TN22 5QE England

Tel: +44 (0) 1825 749494
Fax: +44 (0) 1825 765701

www.naval-military-press.com
www.military-genealogy.com
www.militarymaproom.com

In reprinting in facsimile from the original, any imperfections are inevitably reproduced and the quality may fall short of modern type and cartographic standards.

EDITOR'S NOTE

(*August, 1916*)

SOME months ago a few copies of these letters were printed, for private distribution, under the title of "With the American Ambulance Field Service in France." So keen was the interest that they stirred, and so many the requests for them which followed, that permission for their publication and sale in America was subsequently asked of the *Ministry of Foreign Affairs* in Paris. The French Government, which had conferred upon their author last October the *Croix de Guerre* for valor, has now given the necessary sanction and approval. The preface and introduction, written for the original edition, have been left here unaltered, as they explain the circumstances to which this book owes its existence. The title only, for brevity's sake, has been changed to "Ambulance No. 10."

FOREIGN AFFAIRS
Office of the Minister

Paris, August 14, 1916.

*M. Berthelot, Ministre Plénipoten-
tiaire, Chef de Cabinet du Ministre des
Affaires Etrangères, Président du Conseil,
after having read with interest Mr. Leslie
Buswell's book, " With the American Ambulance Field Service in France," considers
that the public sale in the United States of
so excellent a record can only prove advan-
tageous, and he desires to state that, in be-
half of France, the censor finds nothing to
suppress.*

[signed] BERTHELOT

Paris 14 août 1916

M. Berthelot, Ministre plénipotentiaire,
chef du Cabinet du Ministre des affaires étrangères
Président du Conseil, après avoir pris
connaissance avec intérêt du livre de
M. Leslie Boswell "With the ~~ambulance~~
American ambulance field service in France,
estime qu'il n'y a que des avantages
à mettre en vente cet excellent
récit aux États-Unis et, en ce qui
concerne la France, déclare qu'il
n'a rien à supprimer.

Pour le Ministre et par autorisation,
Le Chef du Cabinet et du Personnel

Berthelot

PREFACE

THESE letters, according to ordinary ethics in such matters, should not, perhaps, be published. They were merely intended as tributes of friendship and remembrance. Casually written — in pencil often — at moments between duties, with no thought of their being destined to any further purpose than that distance and absence might count a little less through the pictures they would give of a day's work far away.

Excepting that here and there in each letter a few details quite personal have been omitted, and of course the names of places sometimes changed, they are untouched. Their author has had no chance to revise them, nor, it must be confessed, has his consent to their printing been asked.[1] Knowing him, there seemed little

[1] This, of course, has now (Aug., 1916) been granted.

likelihood of his believing them worthy of
special attention; not at least without a
correspondence of persuasion, and much
loss of time. Only the exigency of the
hour and a conviction of their worth have
led me to take this step. If they give to
those who may now read as clear a vision
as they have given me of the chivalrous
work our young American volunteers are
doing in France, they will have achieved
something. If occasionally, some reader
— grateful for this proof that our country
is contributing so worthy a part to the
heroism of to-day — should feel inspired
to do what he is able toward the encouragement and continuation of this work,
these letters will have served a high purpose. The knowledge that a possibility so
worth while would ultimately outweigh
with my friend any personal considera-
tion is justification of the liberty taken
— and of this book.

Perhaps for the time and effort the

writer of these records so generously spent for friendship's sake in the midst of hard and hazardous days he may find recompense in the realization that, aside from the pleasure which their coming meant to one who looked for them, they may bring much benefit to " the Service " he so valiantly describes, and through that service, to thousands of men and women whose happiness death might otherwise have destroyed.

H. D. S.

GLOUCESTER, MASSACHUSETTS
September 15th, 1915

ILLUSTRATIONS

LESLIE BUSWELL . . . . *Frontispiece*

SOME OF THE SECTION AT PONT-À-MOUSSON . . . 1

BRIDGE OVER MOSELLE AT PONT-À-MOUSSON . . . 6

TRENCH WORK 6

SOLDIERS' GRAVES AT BOIS-LE-PRÊTRE 8

PUTTING IN UPPER STRETCHER 16

LOADING AN AMBULANCE 16

DIEULOUARD 22

FISHING WITHIN RIFLE-RANGE OF THE BOCHES . . 22

POSTE DE SECOUR AT AUBERGE ST. PIERRE . . . 40

DECORATIONS FOR THE 4TH AT HEADQUARTERS . . 44

PONT-À-MOUSSON HOUSE HIT BY A "210" . . . 50

BURNING CHURCH AT PONT-À-MOUSSON STRUCK BY IN-
CENDIARY SHELL 56

MONTAUVILLE 56

HOUSE IN WHICH LARGE HOLE WAS MADE BY A SHELL 76

THE SNAPSHOT OF A GERMAN FIRST LINE TRENCH FROM
A FRENCH ADVANCE POST 84

HOUSES AT PONT-À-MOUSSON 92

CEMETERY AT PONT-À-MOUSSON 102

VIEW OF MOSELLE BEHIND MY HOUSE   106

QUART-EN-RESERVE   106

GRENADE CATAPULT, FIRST LINE TRENCHES   .   .   . 132

MAIN STREET OF FEY-EN-HAYE   140

THE WRECK OF THE GERMAN AEROPLANE 144

INTRODUCTION

FOR many years before the war there existed at Neuilly-sur-Seine, a suburb of Paris, a semi-philanthropic institution supported by Americans and known as the American Hospital. At the outbreak of the war this institution instantly and naturally became the rallying-point for Americans who loved France and wanted to help care for her wounded soldiers. Within a few weeks it was evident, however, that larger quarters must be found. A splendid new school building, which was rapidly nearing completion in the neighborhood, was rented; its large, well-lighted, and well-ventilated rooms were transformed into hospital wards, operating-rooms, dormitories, and offices; a multitude of doctors, surgeons, and nurses were brought over from the United States;

and thus the American Ambulance Hospital in the Lycée Pasteur, with accommodations for more than six hundred wounded soldiers, came into being. Soon the generosity of another American friend of France made possible a second American Ambulance Hospital, and the venerable College of Juilly, located about thirty miles east of Paris, was steam-fitted, electric-lighted and plumbed, and made over into a hospital for about two hundred additional wounded, with distinguished American surgeons in charge.

From the outset it was clear that the saving of soldiers' lives depended quite as much upon the quick transportation of the wounded as upon their surgical treatment, and in September, 1914, when the battle front surged close to Paris, a dozen automobiles given by Americans, hastily extemporized into ambulances, and driven by American volunteers, ran back and forth night and day between the western

end of the Marne Valley and Paris. This
was the beginning of the American Ambulance Field Service with which the following letters have to do. During the autumn
and winter that followed many more cars
were given and many more young Americans volunteered, and when the battle
front retired from the vicinity of Paris,
sections of motor ambulances were detached from the hospitals at Neuilly and
Juilly and became more or less independ-
ent units attached to the several French
armies, serving the dressing-stations and
Army hospitals within the Army zone.
To-day more than a hundred such ambulances given and driven by American
friends of France are carrying wounded
French soldiers along the very fighting
front in Belgium and France.[1]

In Belgium and Northern France,
where the American Ambulance Field
Service has had an important Section since
the early months of the war, the valiant

[1] There are at present (1916) over two hundred.

service rendered during the second battle of the Yser, and during the many bombardments from long-range guns in and about Dunkirk, has attracted official recognition from the highest officers in the Army. At the time of the prolonged battles in the vicinity of Ypres in May, General Putz wrote that the American Section had, by working five nights and days without interruption, assured the evacuation of the hospitals in Everdinghe, though under continual shell fire which covered all of the roads in the neighborhood and even the hospitals themselves. "I cannot praise too highly," he added, "the courage and devotion of which the men in your Section have given evidence, and I ask you to transmit to them my congratulations and my thanks for the great physical effort which they have so generously made and the signal services which they have rendered."

In the section of Alsace which France

has definitely recovered from Germany,
the American Ambulance Field Service has
now the only automobile ambulances and
they are performing a service which no
other automobile ambulances could per-
form. Because of the lightness and power
of our little cars, and because we are willing to use them up in this service and replace them without restrictions, our ambulances are running over steep mountain
passes in Alsace which the French auto-
ambulances are unable to cross and over
which wounded soldiers were formerly
carried on mule-back. They have been
able to reduce the duration of the journey
of the wounded between the dressing-stations and the hospitals from four or five
hours to less than one, at the same time
substituting transport in a comfortable
springed vehicle for the agony of transport
in the mule-litters. Two of the men in this
Section have already received the "Croix-
de-Guerre" for special acts of valor.

We have another Section of ambulances attached to an American army field hospital of thirty tents, which is also a branch of the American Ambulance Hospital made available to the French Army by generous American friends. This movable hospital is equipped to care for one hundred and forty wounded, and the whole installation of ward tents, officers' and nurses' tents, operating-tents, mess-tents, etc., can be mounted by our men or demounted and packed on motor-trucks ready for transportation in less than three hours. It is destined to be of great service in the devastated regions when the French Army begins its advance.

Finally, we have a Section of ambulances in Lorraine to which has been entrusted exclusively the service of carrying the wounded in the much-fought-over region around Bois-le-Prêtre. This Section alone has carried on the average about seventy-five hundred wounded per month.

The men work continually within range of
the German shells and are almost daily
under German fire. The Section as a
whole, and their leader, have received
honorable mention in official dispatches
and have been given the "Croix-de-
Guerre."

The daily life and activities of the men
of this section are sketched by one of
its members in the following personal letters, which — while written without any
thought of publication — are now pri-
vately printed in order that those generous Americans on the other side of the
Atlantic who are making this chivalrous
work possible may more truly appreciate
its value and efficiency. From this unconscious story one gets an impression of the
devoted service which young Americans
are rendering in France and of the way
in which they are reducing the agony and
saving the lives of wounded French soldiers. One sees, too, how deeply this serv-

ice is appreciated, and how through it the old friendship which has existed between France and the United States since the very beginning of our national history is being quickened and rejuvenated.

" Happy are all free peoples, too strong to be dispossessed,
But blessed are those among nations who dare to be strong for the rest."

A. P. A.

September 6, 1915.

SOME OF THE SECTION AT PONT-À MOUSSON

"Lord, Thy most pointed pleasure take
And stab my spirit broad awake."

Stevenson

AMBULANCE NO. 10

PERSONAL LETTERS FROM THE FRONT

AMERICAN AMBULANCE, *June 17th.*

I CAME here — Pont-à-Mousson — last night after a seven hours' journey to Nancy from Paris. On the way I found much to interest me, as (if you will look on your map) you will see that the railway runs beside the River Marne, then the Meuse, and lastly the Moselle. An officer pointed out to me all the interesting places where the Germans advanced and then re-treated in a hurry, — or practically a rout, — leaving everything behind even to their flags, which I believe are now in London. After passing these and nearing Nancy I saw what looked like a fleet of aeroplanes, and the officer explained to me that it was a flying Taube being shot at by the French. It looked like this: —

I am told that they rarely hit one.

On arriving at Nancy I was met by Salisbury, our Section leader, and after a very good meal in the most beautiful little town you could hope to see (and where the Kaiser and ten thousand troops in dress parade were waiting on a hill close by to enter in state last October), we started by motor for Pont-à-Mousson. Some fifteen kilometres farther on, our lights were put out and we then entered the region under

shell fire. It was a funny feeling listening
to my conductor talking about how this
shell and that shell hit here and there; and
all along the route we passed torn-up
trees, houses, and roads. At last we came
to Pont-à-Mousson, a dear little village
with about eight thousand inhabitants,
and felt our way, so to speak, in the darkness and silence to the barracks which are
now the Headquarters of the Ambulance.
I found that there were about twenty cars
and twenty-two men here, the latter all
enthusiastic about their work and the help
the Section were giving the French. The
day before I arrived a shell hit the house
next door, and on first sight one would
think it was the barracks itself which had
been hit. These huge high-explosive shells
are sent into the town every two or three
days, and everywhere one sees masses of
brick and stone, all that remains of houses
struck. The Germans have bombarded
the town over one hundred and ten times.

After being introduced to the "boys," I went to my room which is some one hundred and sixty metres up the road — nearer the trenches, but safer for all that. Here I found I was to share the house with another man, Schroeder by name, a Hollander and a very nice fellow, who has already lost one brother and has had another wounded in the French army. My bedroom is a quite typical French peasant room, very comfortable, and I felt grateful to know that I was to have a bed and not straw to sleep on. I went to sleep there my first night in comparative quietness, only hearing now and then a crack of a musket which in peace time one would think was merely a back-fire of some motor. In the morning I woke at six and went to breakfast in our barracks, which is always served at seven o'clock. Walking out of my front door I came into the main street. To the left is the way to the town and the barracks — to the right the road goes straight on, an avenue of trees. My friend or housemate pointed out, about five hundred metres away, what looked like a fallen tree across the road. Imagine my feelings when he told me that they were the French trenches. To the right and left of this avenue are hills and on the left runs the River Moselle. On the ridge of hills on the right, one sees a brown line — these are the German trenches, and walking down the road to breakfast, one gets the knowledge that a first-class rifle shot could pick one off. After breakfast I was asked by one of the men, Roeder, if I would like to look about the place, and I jumped at the invitation. We got into a Ford Ambulance (no one can realize the excellence of the Ford for this purpose until he has seen what they can do), and we started on a tour, or "petit promenade," as an officer told us we were doing.

Pont-à-Mousson was in the hands of

the Germans for five days and our Headquarters were the German Officers' Headquarters. The French partially blew up the bridge which crosses the Moselle at this most picturesque point, and for the last five days the Germans have been bombarding it, attempting in their turn to destroy it; many of the houses round it seem to have been hit, and the two places where shells have taken most effect are on the bridge the French have repaired with wood. The boys tell me it is a wonderful sight to see the water rising like a geyser when the shells hit in the river. To show how careless the few remaining peasants are, directly the Germans have "apparently" ceased firing, they get into boats to pick up the fish killed in hundreds by the concussion. We left the river (where we could be clearly seen by the Germans entrenched some thousand metres away), and I confess I sighed in relief — for it is difficult to accustom one's self immedi-

BRIDGE OVER MOSELLE AT PONT-À-MOUSSON

TRENCH WORK

ately to the possibility of receiving a
bullet in one's head or a shell in one's
stomach. We then went through the town,
everywhere being told stories of how, on
such and such a day last week, five men
were killed there and three wounded here,
etc. All the houses are left open, and one
can walk into any doorway that looks
interesting and do a tour of inspection.
We left Pont-à-Mousson and started up
the hill to our first " place de secour " —
X—— — you will see it on your map
some three kilometres from Pont-à-Mousson. Roeder, as we sped on, carefully
explained that I was never to drive along
this particular road, but was to take a
back way, as the Commandant had for-
bidden any one to use this route which
was in full view of the German artillery
and trenches. If he could have realized
how I felt, he would have taken me by the
back way that time too.

*   *   *   *   *   *   *

On the other side of the hill on our right extended the famous Bois-le-Prêtre; but it is no longer a wood — it is just a wilderness with a few brown stumps sticking up. "Would you like to go into the Bois?" I was asked. I felt I had been in as much danger as I was likely to get into, so I said yes, and we turned to the left and mounted a steep hill and entered it. Here the birds were singing and all was green and beautiful (it was a part where the artillery had not been) but one could see trench after trench deserted. Here was an officers' cemetery, a terribly sad sight, six hundred officers' graves. Close by were also the graves of eighteen hundred soldiers. The little cemetery was quite impressive on the side of this lovely green hill with the great trees all around and the little plain wood crosses at each grave. As we waited a broken-down horse appeared with a cart-load of what looked like old clothes — "Les Morts." I had never seen

SOLDIERS' GRAVES AT BOIS LE PRÊTRE

a dead body until that moment. It was a
horrible awakening — eight stiff, semi-
detached, armless, trunkless, headless
bodies, — all men like ourselves with people loving them, — somewhere, — all gone
this way, — because of — what? I don't
know, do you? A grave had been dug two
metres deep, large enough to hold sixteen,
and then we were asked to group ourselves
around the car to be taken "pour sou-
venir." I managed to do it. I stood there
by those dead men and tried to look as if it
were a natural thing to do. I felt like being sick. Then one by one they were low-
ered into the grave, and when they were
all laid out the identification started to
take place — the good boots were taken
off — and if a coat was not too bloody or
torn it was kept — "Surely we must be
going," I said. "No, no! not before we
have shown you the dead in the *fosse*
there." "Good God," I cried, "I can't do
that now"; and I did n't. We returned

to Pont-à-Mousson for lunch at twelve o'clock and I felt a very different person — and wondered how I could have felt faint the week before on merely seeing the photographs of wounded in our Neuilly Hospital; — one becomes "habitué," they tell me. I was then officially handed over the car I am to drive, and I began looking over all the parts, as we have to do everything for ourselves here.

Saturday.

It hardly seems possible that we are so close to the German trenches — fair food — even hot water — wonderful moonlight nights, and a comfortable bed. Every other night we have to sleep in barracks to be on duty any moment, and so we sleep on straw and don't undress. Every fourth night we are on duty all night and go to X—— and stay there in the car taking wounded to the first, second, and third base hospitals.

Thursday was my baptism of fire, for we had a great artillery duel, and it was very interesting, though not at all quieting to hear the big guns fired and shells exploded over our heads. About six o'clock it stopped and we went in to dinner. Afterward another boy — Barclay — went for a walk with me, and we stopped to talk to two peasant girls who still remained in the town. "Come in and have some strawberries," they invited. And the way these girls offered us all the little luxuries their house could afford showed us how respected the American Ambulance is by the peasants as well as the officers. "Do you fence?" one of them asked. "Yes, a little," I answered, and foils were brought out and we started in. The girl fenced well, but I managed to remember a little of what I once knew, when suddenly I heard a man's voice say in French, "Well done, well done — give me the foils, my daughter, quick"; and I was introduced to a fine old soldier who had fought in the campaign of 1870. We saluted and started again, but here I soon realized the touch of a master, and although I got in a few hits I was easily beaten and felt a little downcast. "But my husband is a professor of fencing for forty years," observed Madame. I retired to bed, feeling that though beaten I might have many happy games in the evening at fencing with the "vieux maître." Yesterday I took out my ambulance alone and carried eight wounded for the first time. I am now gradually slipping into my place and the sense of strangeness is passing off.

June 19th.

To continue from where I left off — I am now on duty at the Bureau — our Headquarters here. Last night as I was finishing my dinner I was told to go to F—— to fetch a contagious case and take it to the train.

Sunday.

I was suddenly interrupted by being called to fetch the wounded from X——— and I am just back.

My roommate offered to come with me to get the contagious case (which proved fortunately to be only measles), and we started off on what I thought then one of the most amazing trips of my life. Turning suddenly to the left from the main road, I drove our little Ford three kilometres along the road, which was in full view of the Germans and which had been the death place of many passers-by, then turning left again we drove slowly to a village so full of soldiers that it seemed impossible so many could even find shelter — a quick turn to the right — up — up — up — first speed — along a very narrow road with just room for the car. On both sides were stuck up cut tree branches to make the Germans think

there was no road. Up we went through
another tiny hill village full of artillery,
and on every side, underground dugouts
where they all live — trees blown down —
branches stuck here and there to look like
trees, and at last we reached the top. The
water in the radiator was boiling, so we
stopped, walked a bit in the most beautiful woods, and picked flowers and wild
strawberries to the tune of birds and dis-
tant cannon. In this wood are heavy naval
guns, but *from* where and *how* they were
ever taken there is a puzzle. On we went
through more woods until we were stopped
by a sentry, who directed us still further,
and then I saw what was the most dream-
like spectacle I ever beheld.

The thick woods teemed with soldiers,
and dotted through the forests were little
huts, very low, where they live — thousands of them — pathways starting every
twenty yards to some new wood village.
We heard music, and on reaching our des-

tination were invited to inspect these
quaint habitations. We walked down a
path past hut after hut, and then suddenly the wood opened out and we came
to a kind of amphitheatre, and my friend
and I were conducted to "fauteuils," so to
speak, and we listened (after much hand-
shaking and "vive l'Amérique," "vive
l'Angleterre," and "camarades," etc.) to
a band of three, banjo, violin, and dul-
cimer (as I write a shell has just exploded
near by. I jumped to see where — about
two hundred yards away and the smoke is
slowly clearing).

We soon left our friends and took our
contagious case to the station. After
passing through wonderful valleys, hills,
woods, and plains we returned home
pretty tired — wondering how such atro-
cities could be taking place in such a
perfect country. We go regularly to
X—— to get our "blessés," and for two
out of the six kilometres we are exposed

to German view and the whole of the way, of course, to shell fire. On my first arrival at this little mountain village I was horrified to see two people lying dead in the road in huge pools of blood. Six German "150's" had been suddenly launched into the village which is full of soldiers, and killed six soldiers and wounded some thirty. Three of the six shots had landed actually in the road itself. Two of our ambulances were in the street at the time and only chance spared them. I asked where the shells had struck, and my stretcher-bearer looked around for a moment and then pointed under my own car, and there was a hole some nine inches deep and two feet wide. It made me feel rather rotten, I must say. Only five minutes before and it might happen again at any moment. I took down three "couchés," as the lying-down ones are called, and had to pass in front of a battery of "75's" which fired as I passed and gave me a

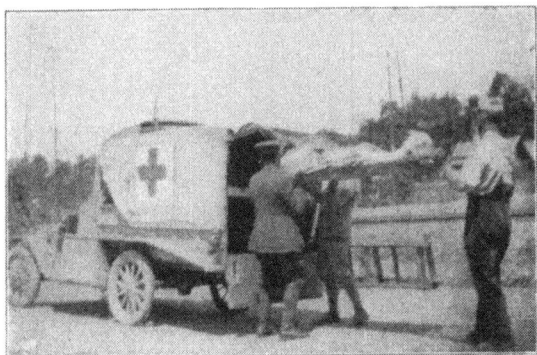

PUTTING IN UPPER STRETCHER

LOADING AN AMBULANCE

shaky knee feeling, I can tell you. Then
backward and forward for two hours
carrying more wounded, and to add to the
excitement it rained so hard that I was
thankful I had bought myself two uni-
forms and could change. To-day is Sunday, and after a rather uncomfortable
night in my clothes and a snatchy sleep, I
have a day off.

Salisbury, our Section leader, asked me
to go with him to Toul, and I went for
what proved to be a wonderful drive
through sleeping villages and semi-tilled
land and woods and valleys. Toul is one
of the most fortified towns in France, and
as we approached we saw trench after
trench and wire entanglements, etc. The
Germans, however, will never advance so
far, I think. We stopped at the aeroplane
sheds where we picked up a Captain
(Australian) and with him entered Toul,
a quiet sleeping town with a lovely
church. Returning we were taken over

the sheds and saw a large quantity of bi-
planes and monoplanes. I am now waiting to be taken up into the trenches, but
the bombardment I spoke of earlier has
continued so heavily that I doubt if we
shall get up to them after all. The whole
Section here does real work night and day
amidst great hardships and no small
danger, and the French appreciation is
very apparent. German prisoners say
that the Germans intend utterly demolishing Pont-à-Mousson if they have to
retire any more, but it would take about
two hundred and fifty thousand shells to
do it and I doubt if it is worth their while.
If any one can imagine the feeling of a
peaceful man who suddenly hears a gun
fired and a shell whistling overhead, followed by the explosion, and then *vice
versa* by the enemy, he will perhaps sym-
pathize with the disagreeable sensation I
experienced when I first heard it happen.
However, for five days it has gone on

constantly and soon I shall become ac-
customed.

Monday.

This very long letter will probably end
in being so dull that it will not be worth
reading, but when everything is fresh to
me it is easy to describe. After three or
six weeks I shall probably write that I
have no news, for one day is doubtless a
repetition of the other, therefore while my
impressions are new I must scribble them
down. I did not get to the trenches last
night, as the bombardment became so bad
it would have been foolish to take so great
a risk sight-seeing. If we had had to go to
get wounded, it would have been different. I stood in the road opposite the little
house I live in and watched the Germans
bombard X——. It was rather like a
stage scene or a colored picture show.
X—— is a little valley town with the
conventional church steeple about two

and one half kilometres as the crow flies from Pont-à-Mousson.[1]

Shrapnel, curiously enough, is not considered very dangerous and the soldiers

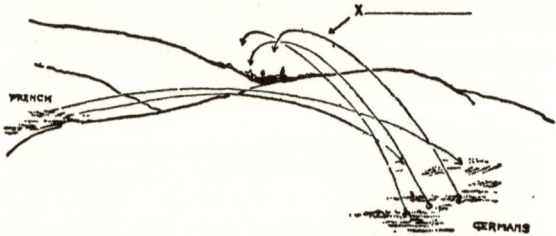

here treat it with contempt. The Germans use it to keep people from going on to the streets to put out fires which may have been started by their "210's" or "150" high explosives. Late yesterday afternoon they set fire to a haystack, and the smoke made them think that the village was on fire, so they sent about 100

[1] The rough sketch shows the indirect fire of the opposing batteries. Every means to observe the effect of the batteries is used, such as aeroplane spotters, etc., and these observers communicate by electrical or visual signaling systems to correct the fire of the battery.

shrapnel one after the other over it, and it was most interesting to see the flash in the sky, then a white cotton-wool effect — and finally the sound of explosion. The French behind A—— immediately opened fire and the music began. It lasted about an hour, but as none of our men were wounded we did not have to go up there. After dinner three of us went for a little walk along the Moselle. One can see the Germans about a thousand metres away on the hills, and as you walk along the banks of the river they can see you distinctly, but they don't bother to fire, which is kind of them! We sat down and watched two soldiers fishing, and I took a photo of them, as I thought it so amusing for people to fish under the direct and easy rifle shot of the Boches. We then went and talked to a lot of soldiers about to return to the trenches. They are all nice to us, and it would make an American proud if he could see how the American boys here are respected and loved. One officer was very indignant because those "dirty Boches" had actually thrown five shells into his trench yesterday! As he wandered off muttering, "*I* will *show* them! les cochons — les cochons — cochons," rather sleepily, I thought — I could n't help remembering the Dormouse in "Alice in Wonderland." It appeared that at the particular line of trenches where he was they had agreed only to fire at each other with rifles! In several places here the trenches are only fifteen or twenty metres apart and the French and Germans are on quite good terms. They exchange tobacco for wine and paper for cigarettes and then return and shoot at each other quite merrily. About Christmas or February, I am told, by soldiers who were then here, they used to walk into each other's trenches and exchange stories, etc., but now they have become "méchant."

DIEULOUARD

**FISHING WITHIN RIFLE-RANGE
OF THE BOCHES**

I am feeling pretty sick to-day and rather dread to-night, as I have all-night duty at X——. I am not at all well. It is the hard food we are having, I suppose. Anyhow, I find myself nice and thin again, so your shocking example of gaining weight last spring is now of no influence. "Doc" comes to-morrow and I will give him this letter to post, as it would never get through unless posted in Paris. I have just returned from Belleville where I took three couchés and two assis. One of the couchés was raving and he yelled and shrieked the whole seventeen kilometres. It was horrible. When I arrived at Belleville, where they are put on a train and sent to a Base Hospital, I found that in his agony he had torn off his clothes and broken the hangers of the stretcher, so it was a wonder he did not completely fall on the two men below. Our cars are packed like this —

I do not know what could be worse than having a poor peaceful peasant who, — forced to fight and after perhaps months of agonizing trench life — badly wounded, shrieks with pain and misery as you try to avoid the many bad bumps in the road.

We expect a big attack to-day and we have evacuated all the X—— hospitals. It looks, too, as if they were preparing for many wounded.

Any kind of news will be greatly appreciated. If you do not hear very regularly from me, remember it will be because work is too heavy.

Thursday.

"Doc" has not yet arrived (he was expected Tuesday), so I am afraid you won't have heard from me this week, as he will miss the mail. I am sitting at the window of my bedroom with the sun streaming through on the table and can imagine myself at "Beauport," or the bungalow — but every three or four minutes, *boom!* and then *bang! — boom!* — the Germans firing on Montauville and the French replying. As I sit here I can see the smoke rising from the village, and I wonder if either of our ambulances which are on duty there have been hurt. "Doc" may come to-night, and if he does so I shall make him come to X—— to-morrow, as it is my day's duty there and he will have some excitement. On my right I can see, about a thousand metres away, the German trenches. It is strange to sit at a window and be in such a position, and yet be writing a letter as though we were all together again in Gloucester. I have been very sick, but to-day I am better again and am very grateful for my recovery. Yesterday I discovered that the main backspring of my car was broken and I had to replace it. Imagine me on my back all day, working like a madman to get the job done in time for duty last night. I managed it all right, however, and so feel myself quite a mechanic. My old bus has a horrid habit of running forward when I crank it. I think I have more dread of cranking my car than of a German "obus." Last night I went into the Square to see the civilians leave. There are not a great many left, but the women are a nuisance — morally — and so the Governor is turning them out as quickly as he can. Alas, that they could not have done their part better! It was a sad sight — many, many tears — and some hysterics! The Governor, a splendid old Colonel, came up

and talked with us (there were four of us),
and was eager to hear when America was
to join the Allies. He quite spoils us all,
and anything we want he sees we have if it
is possible. Last night it was amusing to
see his indignation when he learned that
we were paid, as ordinary "poilus" (a familiar term of endearment referring to the
unshaven men in the trenches), a sou a
day (we don't draw the pay!). He gal-
lantly declared that we should all rank as
sub-lieutenants and should be compensated as such, for he added, "You brave
boys do as much as any soldier at the
front and take as much risk." I like the
French gallantry and sincerity. One meets
it everywhere. The officers all salute us
and the poilus all cheer, smile, and "vive
l'Amérique," etc., and I feel that the work
of the Section is real. I have rarely met
a happier lot of fellows and all so good-
natured and generous. You never hear a
hard word. All work for the good cause,

and as efficiency is unity we try to be efficient. I wish you could see this dear old
garrison town with its poplars and bridge
and church and the lazy Moselle slowly
creeping along to quieter and happier
places. Here and there are fallen houses —
and often gaps in the walls — and torn-
up trees. The house next to us has been
hit and looks like this —

with piles of stone and brick all over the
road. I always try to talk with the soldiers (my French is improving, but still
rotten) and I find they have become fatal-
ists. Some of the regiments here have

been filled up several times and I hear that thirty-five thousand French have been killed in the Bois-le-Prêtre. Every day great shells or hand grenades fall into the trenches and many a poor peasant or higher caste of Frenchman is called away. I took three wounded to the hospital this morning from X—— after they had only been in the trenches twenty minutes, having come straight from the Home Base. They talked so hopelessly about their chance of life.

An old chap asked me yesterday if I would like a German rifle. "Well, rather," said I. He promised he would bring it to me at seven o'clock, unless an "obus" hit him. He did not come, poor fellow, but perhaps he forgot his promise. I hope so.

Pont-à-Mousson, *June 25th.*

You will not have received any mail from me this week, and I am very sorry if

I have caused you any anxiety. "Doc" said he would be here last Tuesday, and to our surprise he has not even arrived yet. I am a little anxious about him and so tried to send him a wire to ask if he is well. As yet I have received no answer. The three letters I have written could never possibly reach you from here, as we are only allowed to write little open letters or postals, so I shall wait until he comes before I send them. The last few days have been quiet, but for me full of interest and hard work. I am better, but my illness of the three days has pulled me down a lot and the food is not good enough to allow me to pick up strength quickly.

I have had many long talks with soldiers and they tell me most interesting stories. One told me that he got on such friendly terms with the Germans in a trench ten metres away that he asked them all to put their heads above the trench so as to take their photos, and I have been promised a copy. Also that they promised to tell each other when they meant to attack or blow up a trench. The mining of the trenches is the most horrible method of warfare existing, I think. There seems so little chance — in fact, none. The worst implement of destruction for the trench-livers is the new kind of projectile called a "torpille," a sort of torpedo. It is fired from about four hundred metres and is noiseless, very large and terribly destructive. Nearly all of the poor fellows we take to the hospital have been "*sauté*" by a *mine* or hit by a torpille. The French have developed a projectile of the same sort, and neither side has had them more than six weeks. It has a kind of tail to its head (see sketch) and is shot from a sort of small gun. Of course they shoot big shells of say "210" or "280" into the trenches, and so marvelous is the accuracy of firing that they explode often on the floor of the trench.

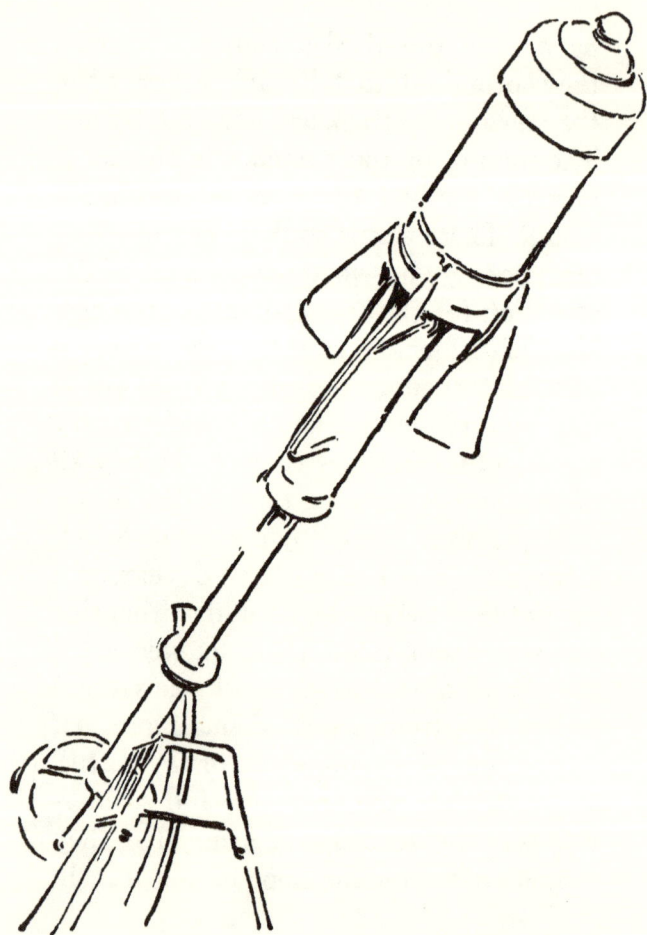

A shell, however, one can hear coming. The whistle is very plain, and you have perhaps one second or two to hide. The torpille gives no warning, is just as large, and, therefore, very deadly.

Yesterday I visited the trenches. I left here at four o'clock in the morning and started up the hill through a little village, rather like what the French call me, "Booseville," which has been much bombarded, and then climbed up past disused trenches until we came to a sentry who directed us up to the company where a friend had promised to meet me. At last I found him and we started for the "premier ligne." I felt a little nervous and anxious, as I did not care to get killed *sight-seeing*. My friend pointed out some bushes to me, and I had not noticed what he said, when on passing within a foot of another bush I found myself looking into the muzzle of a "75" gun. For some distance every inch seemed full of great guns and little guns, all so cleverly hidden that it would seem impossible to know they were there. At last we came to a hill and were told by a sentry that we could not pass that way (for some reason or other — perhaps the position of a battery had just been changed), and we had either to go straight back or right across a field three hundred yards wide in full view of the Germans, three hundred and fifty metres away. Said my friend, "Oh, I think they are eating now; let's risk it. They never fire while food is about." So somewhat against human nature I assented, and we slowly trudged across the open. I confess I was relieved when we reached the shady wood. Still mounting up, we passed hundreds and hundreds of blue-coated soldiers returning from their night vigil in the trenches, and then the noise and chatter of men and birds seemed to die away and I could hear little else but the

crack of some twig one of us walked on,
or the occasional bang of a rifle. This
deadly silence — it was really quite awe-
inspiring — continued as we passed silent
groups of soldiers sipping coffee, tea, or
soup. Then we took three or four steps
down and henceforth walked in trenches,
— winding, curving, zigzag we went, no
trench being more than five metres
straight.

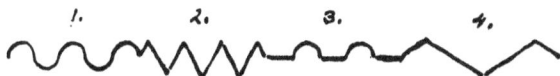

FOUR WAYS OF BUILDING TRENCHES

The soldiers silently smiled, one heard
whispered "Américains." I saluted an
officer, who smiled in return and showed
me his room. Really it was quite comfortable. At last we came to a trench where
every metre soldiers stood looking and
waiting. It was the thin blue line that
guards France's frontier for four hundred

kilometres. The Germans are not pressing or attacking this particular place at present, and so the whole trench is so wonderfully neat and so clean and so uniform and almost comfortable, one began to wonder whether it was only a side show in some exhibition. We walked very quietly along this trench for some two kilometres, and I suddenly discovered that in my interest I had allowed but forty-five minutes to get home if I was to be in time for duty at seven, so I made a hasty retreat and arrived back at barracks just in time.

Monday, the 28th.

Yesterday we heard from "Doc," who wired to say that he would arrive at ten o'clock Sunday night. I have just seen him and he looked splendidly. I soon retired to my room to read the mail which he brought: Letters from you and H—— being the only American ones. Last night I was on duty all night at X——, and

it was a great strain riding backward
and forward in pitch darkness up and
down the very steep and narrow road. I
had to go to Auberge St. Pierre at about
two o'clock this morning. This road is in
full view of the Germans and much bombarded, and shrapnel burst close by,
which reminded me that a lovely moonlight night with trees and hills and valleys dimly shaping themselves *can* be
other than romantic.

It was a sad trip for me — a boy about
nineteen had been hit in the chest and
half his side had gone, — "tres pressé"
they told me, — and as we lifted him into
the car, by a little brick house which was
a mass of shell holes, he raised his sad,
tired eyes to mine and tried a brave smile.
I went down the hill as carefully as I could
and very slowly, but when I arrived at
the hospital I found I had been driving
a hearse and not an ambulance. It made
me feel very badly — the memory of that

faint smile which was to prove the last
effort of some dearly loved youth. All the
poor fellows look at us with the same expression of appreciation and thanks; and
when they are unloaded it is a common
thing to see a soldier, probably suffering
the pain of the damned, make an effort
to take the hand of the American helper.
I tell you tears are pretty near sometimes.
I send you some photos taken by a little
camera I bought, as my large one is too
big. All my love to you and to those who
make the memory of America so dear to
me.

PONT-à-MOUSSON, *July 2d.*

I HAVE just written you a short letter,
but as "Doc" was not here to take it and
mail it from Paris, I could write nothing
of interest in it, therefore follows this long
detailed one for him to post for me when
he comes. Since my last to you he returned
to Paris after being here two days. He

looks very well, indeed, and amuses us by pretending he does not see any excitement here.

As a matter of fact, whenever he comes, we do seem to have a lull in the fighting — why, I don't know — but one of these days he will arrive when something exciting *is* going on. Up to the day before yesterday, one day seemed very much like another — continual explosions of shells— "départs et arrivés" — collecting wounded, etc.; but last Thursday ("Doc" left on Wednesday) we had forty-eight hours of truly hard time. I was on day service at X—— — a little village, as I told you, about one and one half kilos away, of one street about two hundred metres long and one church. I got up there at seven thirty, and, after taking two or three trips with wounded to Dieulouard, was returning to lunch at eleven o'clock, when an urgent call took me to Auberge St. Pierre — a little poste de secour on the

top of the hill past Montauville. I also
wrote you about Auberge St. Pierre in my
last letter — to get there you have to go
on an uphill road within uncomfortable
range of both German and French fire.

On this trip, as my little car climbed
along up the hill, I saw shells bursting on
both sides of the road, and I do not hesi-
tate to say that my feelings were strained
as I entered the wood. When I arrived at
my destination I felt a bit shaken, but the
sight of some eight wounded made me realize that the sooner I got them down to
safety the better for us all. So back I
went down the little winding road to the
sound of shells exploding uncomfortably
near — that was the day's start. Later the
Germans fired fifteen thousand shells into
the Bois-le-Prêtre; the noise was terrific
— almost the whole of our first line of
trenches was plowed up and our cars had
to run all night. About six o'clock I went
back to dinner, but no sooner had I ar-

POSTE DE SECOUR AT AUBERGE ST. PIERRE

rived than a call took three of us back
to X—— and I had another trip with
wounded. I chatted with the "médecin
chef" — a fine-looking man — and he told
me he would give me some photos. My car
was standing outside his little poste de secour, and he asked me a few questions
about Fords in general, while the wounded
were being put into my car. On the way
down, several shells fell all around the road
and I was glad to get back to the Bureau.
Next morning, Friday, we learned at
breakfast that the Germans had sent over
a hundred shells into the little village
of X—— (one street, only about three
hundred metres long, remember!) and that
there was urgent need for our men there.
I went up on foot with Schroeder in the
afternoon (I was off duty) and learned
that my friend the médecin chef had been
blown to pieces by a shell which landed
exactly where my car had stood the night
before. The poor little village looked very

sad, for although a hundred "210's" would not utterly destroy a village, one of them makes a house look stupid after it has been hit. We had been asked to go and see the French "155's" firing, and on inquiring whether it would be safe to go — a smile and an answer to the effect that shells were dropping eight at a time all around the battery sent the three of us back to Pont-à-Mousson.

Saturday.

The bombardment going on now is terrific — I have been standing about a hundred yards from my little house and looked across the valley on Montauville — Bois-le-Prêtre — and watched the shells exploding by the dozens.

Monday, July 5th.

I was called away suddenly — an emergency — and this is the first moment I have had to myself since. I doubt if I

shall ever forget the last thirty-six hours
— they have been so full of work, appre-
hension, and horror.

Tuesday, 5 P.M.

I must write down the events of the last
three days, for I suppose they have been
the most tremendous ones I have experienced. I tried to write yesterday, but
only got as far as those three lines, and
any moment I may be called for "an attack" which we expect hourly. Let me
see — I must go back to Sunday — the
Fourth of July. We had arranged a grand
fête and the Governor, the Colonel, and
the Major were our guests with three
other Captains from various regiments.
An elaborate meal was prepared and all
was decorated — a piano, a stage, and
many flowers, etc. The feast was to start
at seven o'clock, and nearly every soldier
in all of the regiments round here knew
it was the American Fête Day. Suddenly

at about two o'clock commenced a tremendous artillery duel — the whole earth seemed to tremble and the noise of rifle fire almost drowned the explosions of shells — the Germans had attacked!

For some days most of the French batteries had been leaving here for up north where a large army is concentrating, and the Germans (who know everything) attacked us at the most unfortunate moment — and by so doing won back in that short attack much of the land they had lost since December, the winning of which has caused France the loss of over forty thousand men! We all rushed to our cars to be ready for the call, and about six o'clock every car was ordered to X—— — poor little village already badly enough damaged by the bombardment of a few hours before! We worked late and I got to bed at three-thirty, having carried some fifty wounded a distance of about ten kilometres — ten trips — two

DECORATIONS FOR "THE 4TH"
AT HEADQUARTERS

hundred kilometres! In all we carried away over three hundred and fifty crippled wrecks who three hours before were the pride of their nation and families!

Monday, of course, was a hard day's work, for I was on X—— service all night (i.e., two cars stay always in X—— all night for service). I took four long trips in the afternoon and about five o'clock managed to get an hour's sleep, and it was lucky I did. X—— was quiet when I got up there about seven o'clock, and till nine o'clock I chatted to soldiers and then turned into the telephone office to sleep on my stretcher (fully dressed) until I should be called. At one o'clock I woke up to the sound of what might have been an earthquake — the Germans had attacked again and were bombarding X——. We went down into a little "dugout" where we stood listening with strained faces for thirty-five minutes to the shouting of soldiers, the cracking of rifles, and

the terrific reports of French "départs"
and German "arrivés." Literally the
whole place trembled, and when a shell,
probably a "210," arrived in the village
it always seemed to us, poor rats, that it
had exploded in the room above us. No
sooner had the attack stopped than a
phone message came through, "Can an
ambulance come immediately to Auberge
St. Pierre?" — and of course I climbed
out of the cellar, wound up my car, and
drove up the hill. The old car (which was
in the battle of the Marne) seemed to
know it was on a pretty dangerous trip
and it went like a bird. Any unpleasant
shocks of bursting shells, etc., I may have
received on my way up were quickly
compensated for by the greeting of the
Major: — "I wish to thank you and to
congratulate you on the quickness and
efficiency with which you and your comrades execute their orders!" I took four
more trips and at twelve o'clock returned

to X—— and thought I would get a little rest. I was just talking with the phone operator when we saw a flash — and an explosion in the courtyard! After picking ourselves up from the floor where we had thrown ourselves, we hastily returned to the dugout. For three quarters of an hour the second attack went on, and in this dugout, some three hundred yards from the German trenches, the noise was terrific, and I wondered whether I was to be a corpse, a German prisoner, or still a "Conducteur Ambulance Américaine"! When the attack and bombardment ceased, work began, and a general call was sent to our Bureau, and before long, as I descended the hill to Pont-à-Mousson with the first carload of mutilated, I passed our fellows tooting up the hill full speed. We worked until six o'clock carrying down a hundred and eighty or more wounded and then the cars returned to headquarters, as I could manage the few

remaining blessés. About seven o'clock
— tired out — I made a last trip to Auberge St. Pierre, and finding no wounded
there, descended to the next poste de secour, Clos-Bois, and asked if they had any
wounded — "No — none." "But surely
there was a couché on the stretcher
there?" "Come and see: — he is, we
fear, not suitable for your ambulance." I
went up and lifted the covering from his
head and all I saw was a headless trunk!
— "Our dearly loved Lieutenant," said
one of the soldiers, and his voice was not
a steady one — nor were my thoughts
peaceful as I went home to café-au-lait
and some sleep. At four o'clock on Tuesday I woke up with orders to evacuate
the Pont-à-Mousson Hospital (to Belleville). I turned in about two o'clock next
afternoon to sleep again, pretty tired.

Wednesday came the counter-attack.
I must now tell you what we have authen-
tically learned. On Sunday, July 4th,

the Germans made such a successful attack in Quart-en-Reserve and La Croix-des-
Carmes (positions of the Bois-le-Prêtre)
with petrol and gas, hand grenades, mines,
torpedoes, "320's," "210's," and "155's,"
"105's," and "77's" that the French
lost much that they had gained in the
last six months: that they had been taken
unawares, and that we must have everything ready to leave Pont-à-Mousson at
a moment's notice! Next came the news
that Monday, Tuesday, and Wednesday
attacks had been so successful for the
French that they had regained all they
had lost on Sunday ! !

Wednesday was a very exciting day for
me, and I had my nearest escape. We
were evacuating Pont-à-Mousson Hospital
for Belleville (we had not finished this on
Tuesday) and I had three couchés and
three assis in my car. A captain was seated
next to me, wounded in the knee. As I
neared Dieulouard I heard sounds of shells

exploding, and as I reached the outskirts of the town I saw a "210" land in the railway station some hundred yards to the right of the main road. I asked the Captain if he thought it better to wait till the bombardment was over, and he replied, "I must leave this to your judgment, as we are in your car"; so I decided that as the shells generally fall at regular intervals of three, five, or seven minutes (the Germans are so methodical that when you know the time they are firing you can know to the second when the next shell will arrive), I would go on. This time, however, more than one battery was shelling Dieulouard, and as I was passing a house on the road, it was hit by a shell. All was black dust and smoke and I had perforce to pull up a minute — two people in the house were killed, and although my car was covered with brick-dust and débris no one was even bruised! I don't want to come any nearer, however.

PONT-À-MOUSSON HOUSE HIT BY A "210"

I carried over forty wounded yesterday a distance of a hundred and sixty kilos and at nine o'clock turned in to sleep, to be waked up at two o'clock to go to Auberge St. Pierre. Schroeder and I both went, as they had some fourteen wounded and it was necessary to have two cars. It was a glorious morning, and when I got to the top of the hill all was quiet and God's peace seemed to be everywhere. The Major was there to receive us, and so interested and appreciative is he that any one of us would do anything for him. Just as I was starting down with a full load I found I had picked up a nail and a puncture was the order of the day. Two fellows ran forward, and explaining that they were chauffeurs in peace time, refused to let me work on it, and the Major made me sit on a fallen tree by the roadside and smoke a cigarette and talk to him. We are, of course, mere soldiers, but to be treated so kindly and so thoughtfully makes us feel that we must go on forever! The Major said, "You have no idea what comfort and reassurance your cars and your work give to these French soldiers!" I made one more trip to Clos-Bois, where they gave me some coffee and I paid my respects to the bodies of three officers just killed in the trenches. I had a German wounded couché given me and I probed out the fact that there were some six or eight French waiting to be taken. "Oh, but he is seriously wounded — take him first!" When I arrived at the hospital, I watched the German prepared for operation. He had seven bullet wounds in the shoulder, five still remaining, three in the leg, and both arms broken! I picked up his overcoat, and I noticed that the top button was pierced by a bullet, so I cut it off and kept it as a remembrance — a gruesome one, but I shall always remember that in France the German went before the less wounded Frenchman!

Thursday, 4 P. M.

An attack is now going on and I suppose about seven o'clock there will be a general call to X——.

Sunday.

My prophecy about an attack was correct. Now there is a lull again and I have some moments to myself to write about the last three days. Ever since Sunday, July 4th, there has been an attack and counter-attack, and life has been real hell for those poor fellows in the first line of trenches. Every imaginable kind of instrument of destruction has been hurled on them, mines (the narrow part fits into the gun which is a sort of mortar — radius about four hundred metres), torpedoes (radius about four hundred metres) "320's," "250's," "220's," down to "77's," burning petrol, chlorine [1] — all

[1] The Italians, I believe, fire their mortars by compressed air shipped in tanks to the trenches. The direct

this not in dozens, but in thousands and tons. No one can believe what it is like there; it is indescribable, and the Germans are getting the same thing too. I

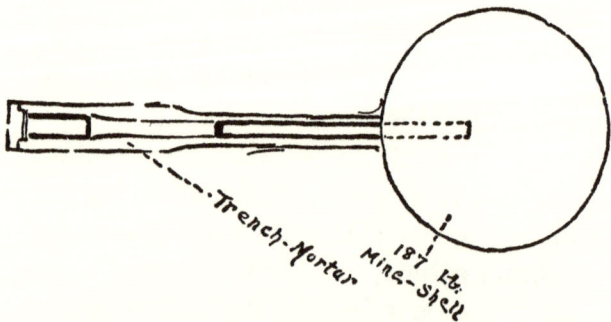

Trench-Mortar
181 lb. Mine-Shell

suppose the French have lost over twenty-five hundred this week in wounded and killed and many prisoners — and this over a line of seven kilometres! And the Germans? Many more! Day and night our Section has gone backward and forward,

reading on a pressure gauge gives the range the mine will be hurled, and the system should be very practicable.

full of wounded and dying, and we are all feeling pretty done up. Yesterday they bombarded Pont-à-Mousson and hit a church which burnt all day, and killed some people — but there are not many left here now and hardly *any* soldiers.

Last night (as after every attack) we eagerly asked how the fight had gone — here we had gained a trench — there we had gained two trenches — here we had not won or lost — but always the same remark, "But the dead and wounded!" At any rate, the Germans are held and our many reinforcements have made the position fairly safe.

On Friday I again took down a German wounded — this time a German of the Kaiser's or Crown Prince's Bodyguard (the German Crown Prince is against us here). He was dying. Picture to yourself a fine, truly magnificent man, — over six feet four — wonderful strength, — with a hole through both lungs. He could not speak, and when I got to the hospital, I asked in German if he wanted anything. He just looked at me and then chokingly murmured, "Catholic." I asked a soldier to fetch the priest and then two brancardiers (stretcher-bearers) and the doctor — the priest and I knelt down as he was given extreme unction. That is a little picture I shall never forget — all race hatred was forgotten. Romanist and Anglican, we were in that hour just all Catholics and a French priest was officiating for a dying German — a Boche — the race that has made Europe a living hell. I came back about seven o'clock at night to the hospital with more wounded and asked if he still lived. "Yes; would I care to see him?" I went in and although he breathed his last within an hour after, his look showed recognition, and that man died, I am sure, with no hatred for France.

I could tell you a multitude of stories — stories so horrible I cannot forget, so pa-

BURNING CHURCH AT PONT-À-MOUSSON
STRUCK BY INCENDIARY SHELL

MONTAUVILLE

thetic that tears are not rarely in my eyes. On Friday night, I was on Montauville duty — and a new regiment arrived — "Bon camarade" to me at once — "How many wounded?" etc., — they asked. I could not tell them that they were going to a place where between their trench and the German trench were hundreds of mangled forms, once their fellow-citizens, — arms, legs, heads, scattered disjointedly everywhere; and where all night and all day every fiendish implement of murder falls by the hundred — into their trenches or on to those ghastly forms, — some half rotted, some newly dead, some still warm, some semi-alive, stranded between foe and friend, — and hurls them yards into the air to fall again with a splash of dust, as a rock falls into a lake. All this is not exaggerated. It is the hideous truth, which thousands of men here have to witness day and night.

Saturday night they came back, some

of those poor fellows I spoke a cheery word to on Friday — no arms — no hands — no feet — one leg — no face — no eye — One glorious fellow I took had his hand off, and although it was a long trying drive to Dieulouard he never uttered a word. I touched his forehead when I arrived and whispered, "Bon courage, mon brave!" He looked at me a moment and answered, "Would God he had taken my life, my friend."

To-day I went to take three wounded officers to Toul, some thirty kilometres away, and before starting I went into the hospital to see if I could do anything for any of those butchered by "civilization." I saw a friend — the man who had offered me a German bayonet. He beckoned me with his eyes and then — "Have they forgotten me? I have been here for five hours and both my legs are shattered." It was true that every bed was full of wounded waiting to be dressed, but I went straight

up to the médecin chef and told him that
a friend was over there with both legs
broken and could he be attended to? "Ah,
we have been looking after the others
first, as *he* must die, but I will do what I
can." I stood there and watched his two
legs put into a position that looked human, and then I bade adieux to a new-
found friend. I think I am glad he will
die. I would prefer to die than to be crippled for life, and if my turn comes I only
hope I may not recover to be helpless.

It is no good trying to make you understand what horror really is — you must
see a bit of it as we see it here to be able
to semi-realize what that place, the Bois-
le-Prêtre, is like. It was known by the
Germans when held by them as " Hexen-
kessel " (witches' cauldron) and as " Wit-
tenwalden " (widows' wood).

I wish you would cut out and keep for
me anything mentioned in the official reports about the Bois-le-Prêtre, Pont-à-

Mousson, Quart-en-Reserve (probably the most mutilated, unthinkable place in the world), La Croix-des-Carmes, etc.

Monday.

I have just received the mail with lots of nice letters. It was so jolly hearing from you all. I am glad to tell you that this Section is to be mentioned by Order of the Army, and it will probably receive the Croix-de-Guerre, which our Section Commander will wear, of course — we may all get some sort of medal some time as well, perhaps. If my letter seems too horrible, just don't send it on to the friends who might otherwise care to hear. My only object in writing so fully is that I do want you all to realize the futility, the utter damnable wickedness and butchery of this war.

P.S. The Governor of the department of Lorraine sent from Nancy the following tribute: —

"On this day, when you celebrate your national independence, at the same hour that France in violent combat defends her independence against an enemy whose madness for domination threatens the liberty of all nations, and whose barbarous methods menace civilization, I address to you the expression of the profound friendship of the French for your great and generous nation, and take this occasion to offer new assurance of the intense gratitude of the population of Lorraine for the admirable devotion of all the members of the American Ambulance of Pont-à-Mousson."

PONT-À-MOUSSON, *July 16th.*

IT so happened that a wounded officer was going to Paris and he posted the letters of July 2d to you for me, and therefore you got them two weeks earlier. Now "Doc" has suddenly returned on his way to Pagny and I am writing about the

last few days. They have been full of
misery and yet full of pleasure. The 14th
of July, the day of the fall of the Bastille,
was to be a fête day for France as usual,
but I little thought I should spend such a
wonderful day myself. Schroeder and I
were invited to pay a visit to the batteries
above one of our postes de secour, and
as we were both off duty, about three
o'clock we went up to B—— in one of our
service cars and thence walked to see our
friends. If any one doubts what grateful
friends and how appreciative the soldiers
are for our little help here, they should
have seen the welcome we were given.
We were shown the "soixante quinzes,"
the "220's," the "155's," and you must
realize by that how completely we for-
eigners are trusted; for could the Germans but know where these guns are, few
of our friends would live to see France win
the war. Next we were shown all over the
"abris" (little dugouts about ten to four-

teen feet underground and covered with three or four layers of good-sized trunks [1] like this). These they retire to when the

Boches bombard the wood. All along the paths leading from one big gun to another were shells, two or three hundred great things about three feet, eight inches high. We then went and had some beer with our friends, all non-commissioned officers, and about four o'clock a corporal came to say that the "155's" were going

[1] These temporary defenses have stood out against shells for weeks, while permanent works were leveled in a few days at Liège, Maubeuge, and Antwerp. High-explosive shells by the thousands are the only answer to field works.

to fire four rounds and would we care to go and watch, as the officer invited us? Of course we followed our guide to the gun and they all posed while I took a photo! Then the officer asked me if I would care to photo the gun being fired and I said yes. I stood some ten metres away, and had just pressed the button of the camera when I jumped half out of my skin at the noise of the explosion. I shall anxiously look for the negatives and I hope they will be good. It was now five o'clock and we had to return to Pont-à-Mousson. Would we stay to dinner — the 14th July? — What! Spend France's fête day with France's artillery in a wood some two kilos from the Germans — surrounded by the guns that were fighting for her liberty? It sounded too good! Of course we accepted; so five of us, three French artillerymen and Schroeder and I, walked down to get to B—— on the road our ambulances travel all day long.

We were all in one line across the road when without warning — *bang!* — thirty metres away earth was thrown yards into the air. The noise was terrific — and then the black dense smoke began almost lazily to fade away. We all five stood still — semi-crouching, although inwardly knowing that all precautions were then futile, — that if we were to be killed by the éclats of that explosion we could not escape: it was too late. After five or ten seconds we breathed again, and I looked at my companions. Three of them had been firing heavy shells for eleven months, but their sunburnt faces had assumed the most haggard, pale expression I have ever seen. I had no looking-glass, but I expect if Schroeder writes his experiences to *his* people he will include my face as being like the rest. Had we been twenty yards farther on — or thirty yards farther back — finis! The éclats of a German shell always go like this —

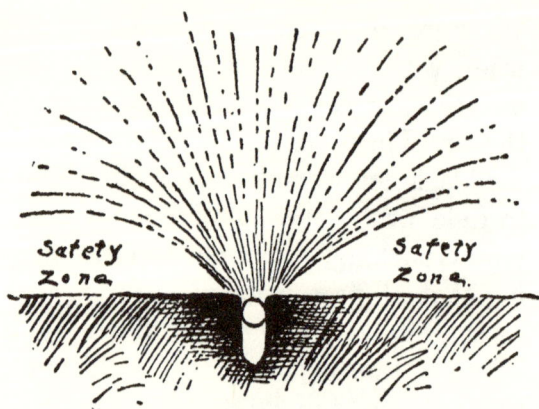

Safety Zone.   Safety Zone.

-German Shell-

but the French like this [1] —

-French Shell-

[1] This effect may be due to the fact that the German shells have percussion fuses whose action is less

The strain made me give a little laugh
which froze pretty quickly on my lips,
for I was silenced with a look — "At-
tends! — listen for the next départ" —
ten anxious ears listened, but it was just a
chance German shell and no more arrived.
When we returned to go to dinner about
an hour and a half later, I asked them to
help me to find the fuse, and there it was
still hot. I shall keep it in memory of
July 14th, 1915. We sat down in that
little wooden shelter, about sixteen of us,
and I cannot tell you what a happy party
we were. Laughter and song fêting the
two honored guests, the "Américains."
The Captain heard we were dining with
his non-commissioned officers and sent up

rapid than that of the French shells. This would allow
them to penetrate the target or ground before detona-
tion, and would give them the geyser effect sketched.
In the French shells, with less delay action in the fuse,
the explosion would take place more immediately on
impact, giving a more lateral burst effect. Of course
the delay in the fuses is easily varied by the gunners.

three bottles of white wine to drink the health of the Allies. We had brought some Moselle as a present to our hosts, and when the others were finished our bottles were a great surprise. They were quickly emptied, a candle was stuck in each and we started singing and telling stories. Then, as an act of courtesy, I was asked to sing our national hymn. I got up (a bottle of wine was fetched to fill our glasses) and did so as loud and as heartily as I knew how. It must have been a strange sight for the casually passing French soldiers, to see their sixteen compatriots standing silently — listening to a man sing a song that they scarcely knew, though one which means so much to so many thousands of our countrymen. I had but finished, when *bang! bang! bang! bang!* — four "75's" fired over our heads — going to kill those who should sing another national anthem. The "Marseillaise" followed and I have never heard it sung in surroundings more fitting or more impressive. Then an artillery duel started, and backward and forward above us went and whistled the shells. Five of our friends suddenly left us, and in three minutes we heard the big "220" firing its death-gift into the German trenches. All the time the songs continued, and those woods must have echoed and reëchoed with the strains of the "Marseillaise," etc. Schroeder and I, however, began to get anxious, for the noise of the artillery increased and increased, and we knew that in about two hours all the ambulances would be needed at X——, so we bade our friends good-bye and arrived home to find that only half of our cars would be required. We then turned in to bed with the conviction that we had really experienced the true feeling of France on the anniversary of the great step toward what she believed would be for the freedom of the people.

"Doc" had arrived unexpectedly from Paris and your letters were very welcome, also one from mother and Mrs. A——. It was the very night, 14th July, that you were giving your lecture. I am *sure* it was a success.

July 15th.

"Doc" and I spent the day together. It was my duty day in Montauville; and although it poured I enjoyed it very much. All we did and saw I shall leave to him to tell you about, so, good-night. God bless you all.

Pont-à-Mousson, *July 24, 1915.*

When I last wrote you I little thought my next letter would follow such a tragedy as occurred on Thursday the 22d. It is now two days ago, so in the comparative calm of perspective, I must try to tell you the whole story from beginning to end. Thursday morning, Schroeder and I went

to visit the hospital on the other side of
the Moselle, and there we were received by
the Sister Superior, who personally showed
us all over the building. The corridors are
now used as wards, as every room but one
in the large old convent has been hit by a
shell. We got back to lunch about twelve
o'clock, and Mignot, our indefatigable
friend in the position of general servant,
upbraided us for our unpunctuality, etc.
We had hardly finished lunch when a shell
burst some twenty metres away and we
hurriedly took to the cellar, while eleven
more shells exploded all around our headquarters, or "caserne," as we call it. We
then went for a round of inspection and
found that the twelve shells had all fallen
on our side of the road and were all within
forty or fifty metres of us. This made us
feel pretty sure that the shells were meant
for us or for our motors. Schroeder and I
discussed the matter, and came to the
conclusion that we did not like the situa-

tion very much, and that if the Germans
sent perhaps six shells, all at once, we
should many of us get caught. I was very
tired, and at about one-thirty went to
sleep and slept until five-thirty, when I
went to dinner at the caserne. The evening meal over, an argument started about
the merits of a periodical called "Le Mot"
(do you know it?) — a kind of futurist
paper. After a rapid-fire commentary
from one and then another of us which
continued until about eight-thirty, Schroeder and I decided to go to our rooms to
bed. We were walking home when I reminded him that he had been asked to tell
four of our fellows who slept in a house
near by to be sure that no light could be
seen through the shutters; so turning
back, we rapped on the window and heard
merry laughter and were greeted with a
cheery invitation to join the nine who
had gathered inside. It seems one of
them, who had been on duty at Montau-

ville, had managed to get some fresh bread and butter and jam, and they were celebrating the event! We had to decline their friendly hospitality, however, as we wanted to get some sleep. I had just got my boots off when — *whish-sh-sh* — *bang!* *bang! bang! . bang!* — four huge shells burst a little way down the road toward our caserne. Thirty seconds after came two more — five minutes later six more — and then we heard a screaming woman ejaculating hysterically, "C'est les Américains." Schroeder and I looked at each other without speaking. We hurriedly dressed and started to run to the caserne — women and soldiers shouting to us to stay where we were; but rushing on through the fog, smoke, and dust, we reached headquarters. There we found the rest of the Section in the cellar, and hurriedly going over those present, realized that two were absent — Mignot, and the mechanic of the French officer at-

tached to us. Out we ran, shouting "Mignot! Mignot!" From the dust and smoke
there staggered some one we did not
know, blood flowing from head, legs, and
arms — "Au secours! Au secours!" — it
was the mechanic. Leaving him with the
Section to be dressed, we rushed madly
through the fog-bound street crying,
"Mignot! Mignot!" Then suddenly —
across the road — a shadow — a dark
spot on the ground — two women quite
dead, a boy dying, a man badly wounded
and — farther on — a still, blue form.
"Quick, old man, listen — his heart!" It
was he — Mignot — and dead. Our loyal
and devoted servant who was almost the
living incarnation of Kipling's Gunga Din.
We rushed back to get stretchers and a
car. Ogilvie got his car and we got our
stretchers out to take away the blessés.
There were a few of us grouped about —
some seven or eight — and a car — with
the wounded just put on stretchers, when

— "Look out!" *Bang! Bang! Bang!* —
three more shells.

We had already thrown ourselves on the
ground, and then, finding we were still
alive, feverishly loaded the car. "Good
God! I've stalled it," said the driver —
then the cranking — would it never start
— try again — thank Heaven, it was off!
Hardly thirty seconds after, *whish-sh —
bang! bang!* two more came. We retired
to a cellar for a few minutes, as the three
dead could stay there while it was so terribly dangerous. At last we emerged and
were about to lift Mignot's body when
both arms moved. Was he alive, after
all? No! it was only the electric wires he
was lying on that had stimulated his
muscles. The car turned the corner with
the three dead and we ran back to the caserne. There we found the rest of our
Section very shaken, indeed. A shell had
burst just outside of the house where
the nine were making merry and the vio-

lence of the impact had hurled all of
them to the ground. Two feet nearer
and the whole lot would have been killed.
Schroeder and I decided we had better go
back to bed, and we insisted that Ogilvie
(who lived in the house so nearly destroyed) should come with us. We made
him a sort of a bed on the floor and turned
in. As the light went out, a strange silence
crept over us three, and I am sure that I
was not the only one who was offering a
silent prayer — for the wife and children
of our devoted friend Mignot, and of gratitude for our miraculous escape from
death.

I must have dozed off when I was awak-
ened by the whole house shaking and six
more terrific explosions followed — and
then still six more! Should we go out
again? No; all the rest were certainly in
cellars and out of danger.

About two o'clock a tremendous attack woke us up, and for an hour the

House in which the nine men were sitting when hurled to the floor by shell exploding just outside. Soon afterwards a shell arrived making the large hole shown — and completely demolishing things within.

whole place shook and reëchoed with the
sound of artillery, hand grenade, and rifle
fire. We stayed awake, expecting a call,
but none came till five o'clock, when we
were told that the "médecin divisionnaire" had ordered us to leave Pont-à-
Mousson immediately. We dressed and
packed and got around to the caserne to
find that nearly every one had already left
and that all thought Ogilvie dead. "Why?"
we asked. His house had been *completely
destroyed*, — even a "280" shell had burst
in the cellar itself. Two shells had burst in
our caserne and all around was wreckage
and mess. I got some coffee at a little
café, and being on Montauville duty went
up there, a sad and depressed being.

That afternoon, about one o'clock, a
shell burst right in the middle of the
street at X—— — killing one soldier
and badly wounding four more. I was
not far away. I took them to the hospital
at Dieulouard, where I found the rest of

the Section getting themselves installed in their new quarters.

In the evening we went, at eight o'clock, to poor Mignot's funeral. Sad and horribly gruesome it was. Imagine a little chapel with four coffins in front of a small altar — one of them with many flowers, and of oak — Mignot's — the other three just pine wood — the ordinary war coffin. The Governor came, and I shall not forget the dim scene — the priest who intoned the Latin burial service out of tune, and the "choir" consisting of one man who sang badly and as loud as he could, and a congregation of silent mourners. Every note, every word, as it re-echoed through the chapel, seemed like the cry of despair of France — a small but pitiful note of the anguish of this country. Over at last, the coffins were shuffled out of the little chapel, and we were allowed to follow them to the bridge to St. Martin, where they were buried in a cemetery constantly upheaved by German shells. Horrible! horrible! horrible! — that is all I can write.

There had not yet been time to find rooms in Dieulouard, and I was asked if I minded sleeping in Pont-à-Mousson. "No, not a bit!" So I spent last night there alone, and perhaps for the last time — in our little room, Schroeder's and mine, of which I once sent you a photo. He was at X—— on night duty.

This morning I am sitting in that room at the window writing this — all's quiet — the sky, cloudless and blue — birds are singing — the red roses in the garden blossom in the sun, and the peace of Heaven is really on earth around me. Then comes the memory of Thursday night; a vision of another world.

"Doc" will probably arrive here today, as we had to wire him at once, and so you may get this letter next mail.

SINCE Friday, things have been topsy-turvy. Our Section leader was away "en repos" and Glover, who is in charge in his absence, naturally feeling responsible for the safe-keeping of our many ambulances in this division of the army, thought best to evacuate Pont-à-Mousson. Of course the point of virtue in the idea was to avoid the possible loss of some of our men as well as cars — which would be a tragedy for the French wounded. But our Section is here to give its *best service* and I can't help feeling that it is better not to lower the standard of work and efficiency by retiring to ——. Perhaps I have rather forcibly expressed this idea, but a number of the men here are of the same opinion. I sleep at Pont-à-Mousson as usual, and of course Schroeder does too, and now three others also. I want to point out that the moral effect of seeing

us about this place is very great on the
soldiers encamped here, and if you could
have heard their condolences and seen
the look of pleasure on their faces when
Schroeder and I walked down the street
last night, you would realize that what
little extra risk it involves is negligible,
compared to its beneficial effect. However, when Salisbury returns, we may
have to leave, for good, dear old Pont-
à-Mousson. I suppose you saw in the
official French report of the 29th that
we had been shelled — it meant *something*
to you then, I am sure — but you little
realized that it was our little group of
ambulances they were hammering at.

Our whole Section has been cited by
Order of the Division, and last night the
official wording, etc., was sent to us. It is
really a very great compliment and I am
so pleased — I expect Salisbury will get
decorated as head of the Section. Here is
a translation of it: —

"American Ambulance Automobile, Section A.Y., composed of volunteers, friends of our country, has been continually conspicuous for the enthusiasm, courage, and zeal of all its members, who, regardless of danger, have worked without rest to save our wounded, whose affection and gratitude they have gained."

Poor Mignot — life at Pont-à-Mousson will be very different without him; and our mechanic, who was wounded, is, I now hear, to have his left arm amputated.[1] What a real tragedy the 22d was for us!

The more we think about the evening, and as further details come to light, the more we marvel that we were not all killed. It is strange, too, how those who one felt would behave well — did — and I am proud of my friends in the Section.

P.S. We hear that a German captain, a prisoner in Paris, said that if any American ambulance man was captured pris-

---

[1] He died soon after.

oner he would be shot! Nice lot of people! are n't they?

July 29, 1915.

I had a very interesting day yesterday; as you will have seen by official reports, the Germans presented us again with some twenty to thirty big shells on Monday night, and although I was at Pont-à-Mousson, I was in a good cellar! About three people were killed, but one woman was wounded, just down the road, and the doctor and I had to run out and bring her in. We were sufficiently excited not to think of more shells, and as she could run too — and did so with a vengeance — it was not a long "promenade"!

Yesterday, I went with Schroeder to lunch with the battery who had entertained us at dinner on the 14th July. They had moved their position nearer the Germans. I have rarely enjoyed a day more — the sun was glorious — the views

perfect — and the woods enchanting —
though shells bursting in the air took the
place of birds! We had a splendid lunch,
and afterwards went out and visited the
numerous guns and trenches. I took
many wonderful photos (*c'est à dire* they
ought to be), I saw about five different-
sized guns, and then we advanced to the
trenches. Finally we reached the first line,
where silence reigned supreme except for
the occasional bang of a rifle or the inter-
mittent explosion of shells. We went to
an advanced post (several metres in front
of first line), and there carefully looking
through a hole I saw the German trenches.
I then expressed a wish to be able to photo
them, and I was shown a place where I
could stand up and quickly get a snapshot. I regretted having made the wish,
but I saw they were looking at me, and I
did n't intend showing a white liver, so up
I jumped and took two. The bullets did
not whistle all around me, as I suppose I

THE SNAPSHOT OF A GERMAN FIRST LINE TRENCH
FROM A FRENCH ADVANCE POST

ought to write, and although I was successful in taking the picture I do not intend to try the game again.

In fact, I have now seen all the trench
life I want to — and do not mean to visit
them further. The point is that if I
should be killed or wounded on a sight-
seeing expedition it would not be very
creditable, and we run quite enough risk
when on duty.

Strange to say, I felt far less nervous
in the first-line trenches than when on
service at Pont-à-Mousson or Montauville — in fact I felt quite a sense of se-
curity in those splendidly built trenches,
while in a town the shelling is so much
more dangerous; and when you have to go
out into it sitting on that little Ford jos-
tling its way over the bumpy road, the
sensation is not a very comfortable one.
However, as I told you before, I am a
fatalist now — absolutely.

We made our way slowly home to Pont-à-Mousson and there saw shells bursting over a little town in the valley and I got a photo of it. I am tired, so good-night.

July 30th.

All your letters from July 4th to July 15th have just arrived, and also a very nice one from Marconi. It was a great joy to me to know of your success and of your glorious effort. Things are gradually quieting down here, but we have had a *dreadful* time. However, I am glad the work we are doing is so well worth the cost. One has little time and less inclination, in the presence of such great tragedy, to consider the virtue of one's personal service, but somehow it is good to remember that, although one has done work at the front, it was without pay, titles, etc. — I acknowledge that I look forward to October when I plan to go back for a bit. I shall have had four months' service at the front, without a rest, and although I can, I hope, keep going another eight or ten weeks, I feel that without some respite the winter would finish me, if the Germans omitted to do so. I find myself feeling an intense — though futile and unphilosophic — resentment at my physical condition: the not being able to eat enough to keep always at top speed — and of course one can never allow even a shadow, much less a mention of one's own problems to appear. The personal equation practically does n't exist here.

August 2d.

Salisbury, who has returned to us, has supported our little group, who objected to the evacuation of Pont-à-Mousson. He found us a very fine, suitable house (an æsthete would go mad in it — German, and bad German at that), and we were told that no shell had fallen near it for nine months, so we entered with confidence. The telephone was established, and after changing the furniture about, altering a few details, and (I confess it) bringing in a few flowers from the garden, we found ourselves almost magnificently installed.

Yesterday, the 1st of August, the French violently bombarded a town where a German regiment was en repos, and when I arrived at Montauville for day duty at seven-thirty yesterday morning, I was told that all the towns around here were expecting a bombardment in revenge. Needless to say, it was correct.

About ten o'clock I had a call to go to Auberge St. Pierre for two seriously wounded, and when I arrived there, the médecin chef told me that if I got them to the hospital quickly, they would have a chance of living. So "No. 10" tooted off down the hill — at what the plain warrior would term — "a hell of a pace." As I entered Montauville I saw no one about, but as I passed a poste de secour, a doctor rushed out and told me to take two more if I had room. I noticed they filled my car with extraordinary speed, and it was not necessary to tell me that Montauville was being bombarded. My stretchers filled, I set off again for my destination with the four seriously wounded. I decided to take a different road, which was quicker, though supposed to be more dangerous, and two big shells fell on the road I did *not* take while I passed. I began to think myself lucky.

As I entered Pont-à-Mousson, I saw no one about (a bad sign), and on turning to go to Dieulouard where we take the wounded I saw a huge shell explode two hundred metres down the road I was to drive along. Had the ambulance been empty, or with only slightly wounded, I should have waited, of course, but under the circumstances my duty was to go on as fast as I could. I noticed ahead of me

three large motor-trucks and the thought
struck me: "What if those are hit and
contain ammunition." I was ten yards
away when — *bang!* — I was half blown
out of my seat — a shell had landed on
the motor-truck. Hardly believing I was
not hit, I increased my pace and emerged
from the smoke and blackness, going at a
good clip, safe and sound, but shaken. I
deposited my wounded and started to return, but was stopped and told that the
road was not passable as thirty large
"210's" had fallen on it and trees were
all over the place. I forgot to mention the
truly gruesome part of the tale — when
I arrived at Dieulouard, I noticed that
everybody was pointing at my car. I supposed it was because we looked so smoke-
grimed; but on arrival at the hospital,
several people ran out to me with curious
expressions, and I then got down to discover what was troubling them. One of
the poor fellows had thrown himself off

the stretcher and all of his bandages had slipped and a trail of red was flowing from the car and leaving a pool on the ground.

I got back to our Bureau about twelve o'clock by a roundabout way, and had lunch and went up about twelve-thirty to Montauville again.

While at lunch the shells continued to fall at fairly regular intervals on the road. Suddenly those nearest the window threw themselves on the floor (an action familiar to us constantly under shell fire), and before you could sneeze, the lot of us did likewise, and we heard an éclat fly over the house. Laughing, we got up — we were about eight hundred metres from where the shells were bursting — and I went out into the street to see where the éclat had fallen. There it was on the road, weighing about three and a half pounds — it was hot to the touch—three and a half pounds thrown eight hundred metres. I have kept it as a paper-weight — as a little luncheon incident it is entertaining.

Nothing of great interest happened during the afternoon, except that I broke my foot-brake and to-morrow must put in a new one. After dinner, being off duty, I went to bed about eight o'clock. Schroeder left yesterday to go and see his brother who is wounded — he returns in about a week. Meanwhile, I am alone and don't like it. At one-thirty o'clock this morning I woke up. Something was wrong. *Bang! Bang! Bang! Bang!* Pont-à-Mousson being bombarded, and *badly* — fifteen shells falling in three minutes, I counted, and the firing continued for an hour and a half with intervals.

I got dressed — prepared to descend into the cellar if the shells came too near my house, and then about six-fifteen the bombardment stopped. I left the house to find several fires started around the town — they had shelled with incendiary

HOUSES AT PONT-À-MOUSSON

shells as well as high explosives. As I got back to our new headquarters, imagine my surprise to find a huge shell hole — two yards from the house — in the drive itself — the house never bombarded for nine months. All the fellows, however, were safe, and our breakfast was a jocular one, for we could not help seeing the funny side of it all.

August 3d.

Just a few more lines, as one of our Section is returning to America and will take these letters over, and you should get them about *August 18th*, with luck. I hope the lecture was a financial success besides a personal one! If all those people in America only knew what this Section and our work mean to the soldiers here, money would not be long in coming. No one can realize what our little group does for the mutilated wounded — but if any one doubts it, I wish he or she could see the grateful thanks in the eyes of the wounded soldier as he is taken from our ambulance and put into a fairly comfortable bed, with doctors ready to attend him. Let him see the poor soldier, hardly able to move, insist on taking your hand, and let him hear that whispered "Merci, mon camarade" — let him talk to the soldiers newly returned from the trenches or just about to enter there — let him hear that smiling greeting and see those hands waving, "Bon jour, camarade" — let him hear what the officers say — then, if he has had any doubts he could have them no longer. I don't claim that I personally am doing anything, but I do say that this Section of twenty-five men has done more to cement the love for America with the troops around here than any possible action the U.S.A. could take in this war, and I believe that the same fact is true of our Service in the north and south fronts. Every one should realize this, and I hope that any

of my friends to whom you read this letter
will bear our Field Service in mind if they
hear of any one wishing to be truly philan-
thropic. The hospital itself cannot go on
indefinitely supporting us, as they are very
short of funds, and have a great under-
taking on hand to feed and keep up the
Neuilly and Juilly Hospitals — "Doc"
tells me they must get two million francs
to keep things going till next spring. Only
a small portion of that money, of course,
could come to our Field Service, so your
effort is for a great purpose. I must tell
you what happened to the wounded before our little cars came here — we carried
over eighteen hundred last week and more
than seventy-five hundred during July.
They were picked up in the trenches
(Bois-le-Prêtre, etc.) when they could be
got at — sometimes, if lucky, an hour
after, and sometimes five or six hours —
or never. The brancardiers (chiefly artists
before the war!) do this work — a terrible

job, and very, very dangerous, as the wounded are often between the German and French trenches and they have to creep out at night and drag them in. Well, these wounded are carried on brancards (stretchers) down the hill from the trenches — probably a journey of some thirty minutes to the "refuge des blessés" (still in the wood), and there a primitive dressing, to stop bleeding, is put on. Then they are jostled on — on — on — till they arrive at one of the postes de secour, where our light little cars can go — these are at Auberge St. Pierre, Clos-Bois, and Montauville. Here in former days they were re-dressed, and if there were room, stayed in the little shelter, or if not, they had to lie outside till a horse-wagon came to fetch them. Sometimes they would have to wait many hours before their turn came, and even the most urgent cases would not get away and arrive at the hospital for a long time. Hundreds of sol-

diers died thus. Now, with our little cars,
an urgent case is at the hospital ready
for operation in twenty minutes at the
most and generally about ten to fifteen
— no matter *what* time of the day or
night.

That is why these soldiers around here
are so grateful. I have seen cars go up to
Auberge St. Pierre to fetch an urgent case
when the driver knew the road was being
shelled, and the soldiers who see our cars
tooting up the hill, wonder — and say,
"Volontaires?"

I have got a call and so must stop —
for before I could get back the friend who
is to take this letter would doubtless have
had to leave.

1½ hrs. later.

I still have a few minutes, so I will continue. As you know, I almost never re-
read what I write, but I have run over
this letter, and although every word I say

is accurate and unexaggerated, I don't want you to imagine that the French Red Cross is not efficient — but they cannot afford cars everywhere with drivers, etc.; that is why our Section here is so useful. The horror of the whole war is growing on me day by day, and sometimes when I have got into my bed or am trying to get a few hours' sleep on a stretcher (every other night I am on duty and so cannot undress), the horrors of blood — broken arms, mutilated trunks, and ripped-open faces, etc. — haunt me, and I feel I can hardly go through another day of it. But all that is soon forgotten when a call comes, and you see those bandaged soldiers waiting to be taken to a hospital. I almost love my old car — it was in the battle of the Marne — and I often find myself talking to it as I pick my way in pitch darkness — past carriage guns or reinforcements. If one does not quickly become an expert driver, one would have no car to drive, for it is almost impossible to see five yards ahead, and it is at night that the roads are full of horse-carts and soldiers.

August 6, 1915.

I was delighted to see "Doc" to-day. He arrived yesterday evening from Paris, but I was on M—— duty, so we did not meet until this morning. We had a long talk and I told him the story of the fatal 22d; the recital of it only seems to have reimpressed me with the horror of that night.

We are now quite comfortably settled in our new quarters, a house never shelled until just after our occupation of it, when we received a "77" a few feet from our windows. I do not know why it has been spared unless the Boches were anxious not to destroy a creation so obviously their own. Architecturally it is incredible — a veritable pastry cook's chef d'œuvre. Some of the colors within are so vivid that hours of darkness cannot drive them out of vision. There is no piano, but musical surprises abound. Everything you touch or move promptly plays a tune, even a stein plays "Deutschland über alles" — or something. Still the garden full of fruit and vegetables will make up for the rest. Over the brook which runs through it is a little rustic bridge — all imitation wood made of cast iron! Just beneath the latter I was electrified to discover a very open-mouthed and particularly yellow crockery frog quite eighteen inches long! A stone statue of a dancing boy in front of the house was too much for us all. We ransacked the attic and found some articles of clothing belonging to our absent hostess, and have so dressed it that, with a tin can in its hand, it now looks like an inadequately clad lady speeding to her bathhouse with a pail of fresh water.

Last night "Mac" and I were on night duty at M——, and when we arrived at the telephone bureau — where we lie on stretchers fully dressed in our blankets waiting for a call (the rats would keep you awake if there were no work to do) — we were told that they expected a bad bombardment of the village. "Mac" and I tossed up for the first call, and I lost. "Auberge Saint-Pierre, I bet," laughed "Mac." That is our worst trip — but it was to be something even more unpleasant than usual. About eleven o'clock the Boches started shelling the little one-street village with "105" shrapnel. In the midst of it a brancardier came running in to ask for an ambulance — three couchés, "très pressé." Of course, I had to grin and bear it, but it is a horrid feeling to have to go out into a little street where shells are falling regularly — start your motor — turn — back — and run a few yards down the street to a poste de secours where a shell has just landed and another is due any moment.

"Are your wounded ready?" I asked, as calmly as I could. "Oui, monsieur." So out I went — and was welcomed by two shells — one on my right and the other just down the street. I cranked up No. 10, the brancardier jumped up by my side, and we drove to our destination. I decided to leave the ambulance on the left side of the road (the side nearer the trenches and therefore more protected by houses from shell-fire), as I thought it safer on learning that it would be fifteen minutes before the wounded were ready; and luckily for me, for a shell soon landed on the other side of the road where I usually leave the ambulance. My wounded men were now ready; it appeared that one of the shrapnel shells had entered a window and exploded inside a room where seven soldiers, resting after a hard day's work in the trenches, were sleeping — with the appalling result of four dead and three terribly wounded. As I felt my way

CEMETERY AT PONT-A-MOUSSON

to the hospital along that pitch-black road, I could not help wondering why those poor fellows were chosen for the sacrifice instead of us others in the telephone bureau — sixty yards down the street.

However, here I am writing to you, safe and sound, on the little table by my bedside, with a half-burnt candle stuck in a Muratti cigarette box. Outside the night is silent — my window is open and in the draught the wax has trickled down on to the box and then to the table — unheeded — for my thoughts have sped far. To Gloucester days, and winter evenings spent in the old brown-panelled, raftered room, with its pewter lustrous in the candlelight; and the big, cheerful fire that played with our shadows on the wall, while we talked or read — and were content. Well — that peace has gone for a while, but these days will likewise pass, and we are young. It has been good to be

here in the presence of high courage and
to have learned a little in our youth of the
values of life and death.

Pont-à-Mousson, August 15, 1915.

YESTERDAY was a red-letter day for me
— I was made so happy that I feared
something bad must happen to counteract
it. The American mail arrived! — twelve
letters — from H. S., J. H., C. B., C. S. S.,
S——; E. T., etc. — and my uncle and
mother. I wonder whether you people out
there in the sunshine of peace can realize
what a ray of joy and encouragement the
letters you are writing to us here bring.
I got this packet about four o'clock and
being on X—— duty took them up there
to read. I sat in my car with the sun
streaming down over us in that little village semi-blue with soldiers, and started
first to contemplate the writing and the
dates on the envelopes. A battery of
"75's" were firing on my left, and we heard

the shells whistling overhead and after a
few seconds the boom of the explosion on
my right. Even the shells seemed to be singing with pleasure and excitement. Then
I was brought back to actualities by the
voice of a young French soldier — of about
twenty-one — who stood beside me: —

"You just have letters?"

"Yes — not even opened yet."

"All those! You are to be married, perhaps?"

"No, my friend."

"Surely it is your mother, then, who has
written so often."

"Only this one is from her," I answered.
And then a strange silence fell — I did not
feel like speaking, for glancing up, I realized that he was still looking at that one letter in my hand. After a few moments, fum-
bling in his uniform, he pulled out a packet
of earth-stained letters. "These were from
my mother — but I can no longer look for
them — she died last month."

Perhaps it was that little incident that made me appreciate so tremendously these messages from home, but when I got into bed last night and lit a candle by my side to re-read them all, — and when my mother's turn came, — I found the link with that boy and realized how much he has lost and how he must treasure and find comfort in that little batch of memories in his pocket. They too were probably full of anxiety for his welfare, full of encouragement and confidence in his doing his duty as a true French woman's son. And then my imagination wandered to another side: — The letters *from* the front — the letters of assurance — of counsel not to worry — and next, perhaps, the citation — for gallantry — the pride and happiness of those at home. — Finally that most dreaded letter — or the brief announcement in the list of those "Mort au Champ d'Honneur."

Are we really living in the twentieth

VIEW OF MOSELLE BEHIND MY HOUSE

QUART-EN-RESERVE

century after 1900 years of teaching of supposed civilization and Christianity?

The day before yesterday, after having made several trips with wounded, I had a pressing call to Auberge St. Pierre. There the Germans were bombarding as usual, and it was unpleasant. A shell had landed near a kitchen, killing several and seriously wounding one soldier. He had a hole as big as your fist right through his back. "There is a chance if you can get him to the operating-room quickly," I was told — it was eighteen kilometres to the best surgeon; so off dear old "No. 10" and I started on our rush for life. *Toot! toot! toot!* — and even the soldiers, realizing that I had a man's life in my care, made a clear way in the road ahead — and through village after village, without moving the throttle, we sped on and on. *Bump, bump, bump,* — what did it matter if I had to shake him about a little, — he was unconscious, and every second counted. "I hope I won't have a puncture," I found myself muttering from time to time. Finally, I turned to the left — then another corner, — and blowing my horn I drew up at the tent. In a second two brancardiers had the car unloaded — the surgeon in white was washing his hands — and thirty minutes from the time my charge was given into my care, he was lying on the operating-table. "*He may live*," said the surgeon. That was my reward! *That* is why I am happy, even here, — only for this reason, — one sometimes saves lives and never intentionally kills.

The other day I went up to the top of Mousson — i.e., the hill the other side of the bridge. It is under another army division, and so we have to get special permission from the Colonel, but as our Section is treated so wonderfully there is no difficulty in procuring it. We first stopped at the graveyard and tried to find

poor Mignot's grave, but in that mess of
débris, — overturned sepulchres — upheaved tombstones — burst-open coffins
— sun-bleached bones — and the hundred new-made graves, — we could not
find it. We would have continued our
search, but an officer told us not to stay
any longer, as we were in easy view of the
Germans and they might bombard at any
moment. We started to go to the summit.
Up the hill we climbed and the little
mountain-side was all pitted with shell
holes, — some of them most discomfort-
ingly new. At last we reached the top and
began to look about. A few minutes after,
having asked a soldier some question, we
found ourselves surrounded, and rather
roughly asked for our pass. We showed it
with the Colonel's signature, and then
followed a hearty laugh — when they had
to confess they thought our foreign accent
was Boche! We asked in what direction
Metz was, and there just over the hill, to

the right of a little tree we stood facing, it lay, and, like some glorious dominating giant, stood out the cathedral — built by the French for the worship of God and teaching of Christianity, and now so kept by the Germans! — the race which has set loose the scourge. If I could only be in the procession that marches in triumph to Metz!

I must tell you just one more incident. The other evening I was walking down the street when an excited shout made me stop and I saw running toward me an old friend — one I knew when I was in London — now dressed in the blue of France. "What on earth are you doing here?" I asked. "Tell me how in the name of all that's possible, did you get out to the front," he replied, and then we set to and talked. He is a French artist who lived in London and entered the French army, as the English would not have him. He, knowing I had not passed

the "military medical," could not get
over the fact that I had arrived here not-
withstanding. He dragged me to a group
of his friends and we all had a happy half-
hour. Then the usual handshake and au
revoir. As I turned away, he followed
me: — "I go to Quart-en-Reserve to-
night for some days — probably I shall not
return whole. If I am a bit knocked out
you will know, and if I am killed, my people will know. It would be hard for my
wife wondering whether I was *seriously*
hurt or not — she is about to have a child.
Supposing I am wounded, will you post
this letter — it only says that I am getting
on well — am but slightly wounded and
that she is not to worry." I add no com-
ment to the story, but I do wish you could
realize what trench life means to the infantry when they know they have to go
to a hell like the Quart-en-Reserve. I
know what I feel like when I have to drive
along a road being bombarded by the Ger-

mans — but that is only for five or six minutes — but think of five or six days with scarcely an hour's rest out of the twenty-four. No wonder we have to carry madmen to the hospital sometimes.

August 19th.

Poor old "No. 10" has been ill, so I have had her engine down and cleaned it. Now she is running finely.

There is an American stationed here who enlisted in the French army — poor boy, he is only twenty. We asked him to dinner.

"Why did you enlist?"

"Well, I guess I wanted to see some action."

"Are you satisfied?"

"Satisfied? Well, I came here to see life and movement — all I see in my ditch are worms, spiders, marmites, and torpilles!"

"So you have changed your mind?"

"No — guess my mind is the same as when I enlisted — I wanted to see war — I still do. I have n't seen war — I have seen murder and cultivated, systematic butchery."

There has been a lot of "permission" for the soldiers here and they are now returning after their eight days — the first eight days in twelve months, the first time they have seen their wives and mothers for a year, and in many cases they have their first look at their own children born in their absence. One soldier I asked whether his wife was pleased to see him: — "Ah," he said, "you should have seen her cry when I left." "But when you arrived?" I asked. "She *was* pleased! Ah, mon Dieu, you *should* have seen her cry when I arrived."

August 20th.

To-day has been a villainous one. The French bombarded the German stores, and set fire to some large storage-place — we think petrol and stores (perhaps the petrol they spray lighted into our trenches), and from twelve o'clock till now the whole sky has been black with smoke. Of course the Germans made "reprisals" and every little town around was bombarded. One shell which burst where nine persons were sitting dining killed them all.

The telephone bell rings — two cars wanted at once for L——.

August 23d.

About 10.45 this morning a German aeroplane came over the town — not two hundred and fifty metres high. We could see the pilot and observer and the four Maltese crosses on the planes. It was one of the bravest acts I have seen. She was too low for the artillery to open up fire, so the soldiers fired at her with their rifles, and although it seemed as if she must have been hit, the pilot turned around and flew safely back to the German lines. This little incident leaves us with a very uneasy feeling, as we think no German would have taken such risk unless the mission had been very important.

INCENDIARY BOMB DROPPED BY GERMAN AVIATOR AT
PONT-À-MOUSSON

He must have seen everything he wanted to — our cars are fairly conspicuous with their crosses on the top of the canvas. He dropped signals as he flew over our house — and we are wondering just *what* is to follow — and *when!*

August 30th.

The Germans, not satisfied with the reprisals they took on the 22d for the burning by the French of store and factory at Pagny, again opened up on certain buildings of a neighboring town on August 22. They sent over 150 shells between two o'clock and seven. *All* large marmites — 210's, 280's, and I believe some larger. The damage done is considerable, but after such a bombardment it was marvelous that anything remained. Over thirty-three shells fell in the road!

It happened to be my day of repos and I was asked if I would care to go to Nancy for the day, so at seven o'clock in the morning I appeared in full parade uniform, so to speak; and except that I had n't the heart to shave off my temporary mustache, I am sure I must have cut quite a figure!

Off we went to Nancy and spent an interesting day looking all over that wonderful town. Salisbury as you know has got the croix-de-guerre, and we all felt very proud parading the street with him, and his significant ribbon. While the two men with me went to have a hair-cut, which I happened to feel no impulse to do, I stayed outside in the car.

I noticed four Moroccans walking down the street, and casually thought how picturesque their red fezes looked against their blue uniform, when to my horror they stopped by my car and started saluting and bowing and talking so ostentatiously that it took exactly thirty seconds for a large crowd of Nancy inhabitants to collect. The mere fact of being in town for the first time in twelve weeks was quite strange, but to find myself surrounded by a quantity of civilians and the center of attraction was, to say the least, most embarrassing. It was a hot day, and I felt the perspiration pouring down my back, as I looked to right and

left for a way of escape. But my trial was
not over. Horrors! My hand was taken
and all four soldiers solemnly bowed over
it and kissed it. I did not know what to
do — being anxious not to offend them,
nor to add to the amusement of the on-
looking civilians. I thanked them in the
name of America, for the honor they were
paying her! and brought down on my
unsuspecting hand a renewal of the em-
brace. Suddenly — joy! what was that?
An Irish voice! "Sure, young man, it's an
uncomfortable soul ye are this minute."
And an old fellow emerged from the multitude bristling with the hope of a brawl.
However, he calmly joined forces with
me — and we presently left the crowd
with as much dignity as was possible
under the circumstances. From him I
heard *all* about the war, and as much, if
not more, about Ireland, as we sat in a
public house across the street. So ended
an awkward encounter. Well, we left

Nancy about five-thirty (I had bought cakes and various luxuries for the boys), and when we arrived just outside R——, about six-thirty, we saw to our surprise the effects of the bombardment on buildings and the road. Uncertain whether to take a chance or not, we drove nearer and were still hesitating when a shell burst a hundred yards down the road, and decided us! Not being on duty we had no reason to go to Pont-à-Mousson, so turning around we went to dinner at Toul. After a good meal we started home and arriving at my room at eleven-thirty I was relieved to hear that no one had been injured. Several big *éclats*, however, had fallen in our garden and two of our cars had very narrow escapes.

A strange thing to me was the sense of dissatisfaction— of subconscious restlessness —I felt while in Nancy. It was the first time for twelve weeks I had been in a civilized town, where everything was going

on as usual. It all seemed so artificial,
so futile and aimless. As our car tooted
home, I turned around and exclaimed: —
"Oh, Lord! how glad I am to get back
again to our dear old *peaceful* bit of country!" — rather Irish but quite sincere.

The other day I had two hours off duty
and McConnell and I went for a walk
along the Moselle. We saw several soldiers bathing and decided it would be a
good idea to do likewise. It was a glori-
ously hot day, so the fact that we had
no towels was unimportant. I confess I
became "*anglais*" to the extent of insist-
ing on walking along the bank until we
got away from every one and could bathe
alone. At last we found a quiet corner
and started to undress — but we had been
noticed! "C'est les Américains" — and
before we could realize it, some soldiers
were hurriedly preparing to swim in the
Moselle with us, so our bath became a
real party. I only tell this little incident

to show again how ready the soldiers always are to join and talk to members of our little Section.

September 4th.

A sad thing happened the other day to a friend of mine, a poilu who has been helping me to get specimens of perfect, empty German shells (those which have "arrived," but not exploded). The fellow was an expert at dismounting them, — a very dangerous task, — and when he had entirely emptied them, used to bring them to me. I had many a long talk with him, and he got quite fond of American tobacco (poilus don't usually care for "eenglish" tobacco). He used to like to tell me about his girl, and how happy they were together before the war — and how the day peace was declared, he was going to marry her. Lately I had noticed he looked depressed, and one day I found out the reason. I was in his little cellar

sitting on a block of wood, talking of
America, and he of France, when the
postman came to the door. He looked at
my friend — who had become alert —
and shaking his head, said, "Pas encore"
— and murmuring "Salut" to me continued his walk with his precious "letters
from home." My friend became very
white — and presently confessed to me
that he had had no letters for six weeks.
Forty-two days — that seems a terribly
long time out here, you know. A few
days after, I saw him again and asked if
he had heard from his girl. He said "no,"
very sullenly, but later, over a glass of
beer, he mentioned that his father had
written to say his girl had been misbe-
having herself. The poor fellow seemed
stunned with the news. After vainly trying to cheer him up, I went back to dinner. The next morning I did not see him,
being on Montauville duty, but the following morning I was at headquarters

when an urgent call came for an ambulance. My car happened to be just going, so I took the trip. "Where was the house?" I asked. "Just over there where the man is waving." It was the house of my friend. Need I end the story? A broken man, who had worked valiantly for twelve months under hellish conditions to defend his country — had shot himself. We lifted him on to a stretcher — then, feeling pretty badly, and with the doctor's urgent warning against loss of time ringing in my ears, we, "No. 10" and I, sped away to B——. They took him out of my car — read the little pink *fiche* which is attached to every wounded soldier and filled in by the doctor, who has dressed him in the first "poste de secour" — and then exchanged glances. I knew those glances not only meant that life was nearly extinct, but that it did not much matter whether he recovered or not — as he would get six years' imprisonment if he got well, for attempted suicide, and that sentence, in war-time, means constant first-line trench work. I followed him into the operating-room, where he opened his eyes, and I think he recognized me — his lips moved — but I don't know.

The other night came a hurried call to Clois Bois for a poor fellow who had kept his grenade too long and was very badly shattered. "Just a chance if you get him to the Hospital *quickly*," said the doctor. How many times I have felt quite elated at this injunction, and literally flown to the Belleville Hospital; but in this instance I had that horrible sense of hopelessness. It was dark and quite impossible to make Belleville under an hour and a quarter. The poor fellow died before I could get there.

To-day, I took all the carbon out of the car and put in a new commutator. A quiet and lonely day. I feel homesick.

The German offensive which I thought

might take place yesterday did not. The French got news of the fact and of the hour that they proposed to attack, and five minutes beforehand the "75's" opened up and catching many of the Germans already in their first line of trenches so demoralized them as to wholly disrupt their intention. We had only about ten wounded, but goodness knows how many they lost.

September 6th.

I forgot to mention a very important event in the history of the Section. After the Blenod attack Walter and I went to see the damage done. We found the havoc was pretty bad. We were talking to some men who had actually been in a room where a shell exploded and had not even been wounded, when a soldier joined us and speaking in good English, asked if we would like to have some English papers. Although we felt pretty sure they would n't contain very recent news, we had to show an eager appreciation and asked him if he would go and fetch them. We followed him to his lodging. He presently emerged with a large parcel of quite old papers and began chatting with us. London was mentioned and we soon discovered that he had been *chef* for some friends of mine and had after leaving them become *chef* to Lord Fisher. I think I told you that our *chef* was an undertaker before the war, and his cooking was such that we wonder he did not achieve a lot of patrons in our Section. When we got back to the Bureau we decided to ask the Governor of Pont-à-Mousson to allow us to have Cosson — for that was his name — as our *chef*, and of course our request was immediately acceded to; so now we are having food *de luxe*, and the *singe* (as they call the American tinned meat we have to eat every other meal) was quite delicious as a curry last night!

September 8th.

I hope I have not missed to-day's mail. I may have done so, as I hear our letters are kept for some time before being forwarded. In case I have, it will be September 27th or so before you get this, and I shall perhaps have started home on leave; though as the time approaches for me to go, I doubt more and more whether I can actually break away! The only possibility of real contentment now for any one who cares for France or England is to stay until their just cause is victorious — or (as in many a case, alas!) until the call to eternal peace. Every soldier is dreading the winter here and secretly fosters the almost hopeless wish and belief that there will be no winter campaign. However, as day passes day, and all preparations for one go forward to completion, the French, with their wonderful pluck and determination, will resign themselves to the inevitable. The other day a poilu who was standing as usual with eight or nine others around my car at X——, suddenly expressed this compensating thought: "Well, it may be hard for us French this side of Europe, but what a time the Bôches will have in Russia!" — and the idea quite cheered up the little party.

Yesterday I had a sudden call to fetch three badly wounded. One of them was in great pain from a wound in the back, and the slightest jostle or bump I knew would cause him great agony. The doctor, pointing to one of the other two, said, "You must get him to the operating-room as quickly as you can." "But," I answered, "I dare not go fast, *this* poor chap is in such condition." The doctor shrugged his shoulders — but the man who was suffering had heard — "Go as fast as you can, my friend, it won't kill me!" I did so — and the bumps were bad. The poor fellow could not help uttering cries from

time to time. Before I arrived at Belleville, the cries had ceased, as the great
pain had made him unconscious. The
badly wounded man was dead. "C'est la
guerre," said the doctor to whom I told
the story — and I left him washing his
hands for the operation.

I have just heard an amusing fragment.
A German prisoner lately taken, was
seated in the telephone office at Montauville, waiting to be transported. He had
stamped on his uniform buttons an iron
cross, and the French were asking him
why he wore it. He explained that it was
the right of a Section who had earned
the iron cross to do so. The Frenchmen
started chaffing him. He could understand and speak French, and a jocular
remark not particularly complimentary
to the Kaiser was cut short by the prisoner, who, nervously looking round the
room, said in an awed whisper, "Oh! if
the Kaiser should hear of your talking
this way — mein Gott!"

The other day I paid a visit to the hospital at L——, and found all the wounded (only very serious cases stay here) quite happy and buoyant, and the men who had been evacuated in my car never failed to remind me — and thank me. One young fellow about my own age had had his left leg amputated. I sat by his bed and chatted with him, and he told me of his wife — a year and a half married— and of his child whom he had not yet seen. He was so very eager that somehow the pity of it made me turn aside for a second, and look out the window. Quick of perception, out went his hand to mine — "Oh, she will understand, camarade," he said, smiling; "she will love me just the same — she is a Frenchwoman."

How can one help caring for France and French people — they have such keen appreciation of the value of sympathy and gratitude. Here in the midst of torturing death, *they* at least are cheerful, and,

having put aside the barrier of selfishness
are wholly simple and direct in their human relations. The fact that on every
side there is daily evidence of this atti-
tude — in spite of so bitter and costly a
struggle — is high proof of the fineness of
their civilization.

September 14th.

To-day the Section and our Section
leader were decorated. The ceremony
took place in the garden and the "Croix de
Guerre" was pinned on Salisbury's breast.
The double kiss, given with dignity, and
a few words of congratulation to our Section by the *médecin divisionnaire* ended
the notable event. So we now have hanging over our mantelpiece this coveted
insignia.

The Section is not going to move from
here. The General says it is one of the
most active parts on the line, and lately,
although the wounded have not been so

very numerous, the trench bombardments have been so heavy that I anticipate more action.

Did I tell you of the marvellous escape George Roeder and Walter Lovell had yesterday? A shell dropped eight or ten yards away from them in the road and did not explode. I wonder they did n't die of surprise! I don't know what our Section would have done without those two. But everything happens to George and he still has a whole skin, thank God!

No letter from America has come to me for over two weeks, which is not very stimulating. Out here, mole hills are mountains, and mountains — impassable, and although it is of no real importance whether one gets a letter or not, or whether the letter one may get is cold or warm, yet these small and seemingly insignificant things are sometimes enough to send away sleep. I suppose the truth is, I really need a rest and change. It has

GRENADE CATAPULT, FIRST LINE TRENCHES

seemed to me lately that modern warfare means even more of a nervous expenditure than a physical one.

The nights are getting cold, dark and damp. The leaves are falling, underbrush turning — the icy hand of winter stretches out nearer and nearer — and the trials of the poilus are doubling every day.

Yesterday I talked with a priest. He and most of his calling voluntarily accepted at the beginning of the war the fearful task of burying the dead. It sounds very simple, does n't it? Do you realize what it means? It means handling terrible objects covered with blood-soaked clothing, that once had the shape of human beings. It means taking from these forms all articles of apparel that might prove serviceable and searching through these red-stained clothes for any letters or identification. Some of these shapes are hardly of human outline, very stiff and cold. Some are mere fragments,

no longer of any recognizable form. That
is *a little* of what burying the dead means.
I spare you more detail. And this is the
work the priests of Peace are doing in
France. Wonderful, you think? No, it is
French temperament, French courage.

The musician is now brancardier. The
artist, the poet, the paterfamilias of age
past military obligation — all digging
trenches — or any work they can lay their
hands upon. That is why France lives
and has lived through all her agony. How
often have we heard said "Poor France!
She will never stand this great calamity!"
She will stand a hundred such calamities
and always come to the top again!

Sunday.

And for a Sunday, quite quiet. Of
course we had our usual bombardment,
but only shrapnel. About 4.30, they
started to arrive and a call for two cars
followed. I had to go to M—— and on

the way up there, at the X—— I saw a
horrible sight, two dead, three wounded
— and a horse. A shrapnel shell, badly
timed, had fallen exactly in the middle of
the road and made a great mess. Schroeder and Willis were there, so I continued
up to M——, where I got seven wounded.

The American mail has arrived! Letters from you, Joe, and S——. A feast!

Monday.

Serious bombardment of three villages.
Schroeder and I were at Dieulouard, so for
the first time missed it. It was a pleasant
miss for us. Those who pretend they like
to be in bombardments are either hum-
bugs or have never been in a real one.
Having experienced them more or less for
four months, I dislike the sensation now
as much as on my first day.

It is an interesting fact that while the
villages about here are under constant
bombardment many of the oldest civil-

ians cannot be induced to leave their homes, preferring to risk death in their cellars. The other day a very old woman at Montauville had an amazing escape. A "150" high-explosive shell fell into the bedroom of a cottage where she was sleeping. The small room was entirely shattered, but its occupant was not even injured! When I saw her soon after she was in an intense state of resentment over the destruction of her personal belongings, but her own escape did not seem to appeal to her.

I heard a story yesterday which I have every reason to believe is true. I give it to you as I got it:

Early one morning a soldier appeared in a boyau (communication trench) near here in the uniform of a *genie* (French engineer) and started chatting with some passing poilus. He told them he was inspecting the lines and they showed him round their trenches. On his tour, so to speak, he met some artillerymen, who asked him to lunch with their battery. He accepted, and after lunch wandered about the wood with his new-found friends, who showed him the position of many guns. As night came on, explaining he had to return to duty, he left his friends and went to the trenches. It was now dark and on getting to the first line, he told the sentry that he had orders to go out and inspect the barbed wire between the lines. As that was in accordance with the duties of a *genie*, the sentry let him go. The man never returned, and as, on inquiry, the company to which he said he belonged did not know him, there is little doubt he was a German spy.

Another story I heard from a friend of mine in the trenches near Soissons, and it is typical of the hopeless brutality we have to expect.

When the trenches are very close to each other, a little advance post is dug so that one can hear what is being said by the enemy in their trenches. Generally, however, the distance between the lines is too great for this, and at night a soldier is sent out to crawl to within hearing distance of the enemy. One night a poilu so engaged got wounded and when daylight came he was seen to be struggling to crawl back to his friends. Two soldiers promptly started out to help him, but on reaching him the Germans shot and wounded them, so that the three men were now crying to their comrades to come and save them.

Realizing that it was death to any one who left the trench in daylight, the captain forbade more of his men to venture out before dark. As soon as darkness fell, two other soldiers crept forth, but no sooner had they reached the three wounded than an illuminating rocket disclosed their positions to the enemy, and left five men lying wounded between the lines. As the

captain could not afford to lose his men
in this futile way, he detailed two sentries
to shoot any one attempting to leave.
The five men lay there shouting to their
friends — calling them by their names —
reminding them of their friendship — and
asking if they were going to allow their
comrades to die thus without help. So
that when two brancardiers came into the
trench they found the occupants in a terrible state of anguish and nerve tension.
Not being under the command of the captain, and being Red Cross, they promptly
left the trench to save the five wounded
Frenchmen — *Seven* men are still there
between friend and foe, — but at peace
now, God willing.

September 23d.

On Tuesday, Ben and Willis and I went
to Nomeny, a town some fifteen kilometres away, the other side of the Moselle.
It was a long walk.

After stopping to put a wreath on Mignot's grave, we started about one o'clock on our journey. It was a very hot day! We arrived at a little village which at first sight looked deserted. We soon saw the reason. In the middle of the road was a large hole, a little farther on a pool of blood — presently two dead horses — a successful shell.

Passing through Aton the road goes on straight — ever straight — kilometre on kilometre. We passed the village and famous battlefield of Ste. Genevieve on our right. Here, on September 8, 1914, two "75" guns, a few *mitrailleuses* and a handful of five hundred determined French soldiers hurled down an attacking force of 12,000 Germans. Again and again the upright massed line advanced up the hill, to be leveled like bowling pins. After some hours of fighting, the brave little band of Frenchmen on the top of the hill found that they had no more ammunition,

MAIN STREET OF FEY-EN-HAYE

so with fixed bayonets they threw the last advancing Germans down the hill. The latter retired to Pont-à-Mousson with some four thousand of their dead left on the hillside. These they disposed of by throwing into the Moselle. The French lost only fourteen men.

Apropos of this I am reminded of a possible cause for the illness of many of our boys last June. Half the Section are teetotalers, and the other half drink "Pinard," the vin du pays, which comes from the midi and which is supplied to every French soldier. The *water* we were suspicious of, so Ned asked Mignot to ascertain where the *chef* got it. Mignot promised to watch and see whether it really was taken from the spring a little distance from the house, as we had been assured was the case. Imagine our feelings when he announced at breakfast the next morning that the water we had been drinking and which had been used for cooking was drawn from the Moselle!

To continue: A little beyond we came to
the battlefield of Nomeny of August 20,
1914. Along the roadside, dotted all over
the field, are little white wooden crosses,
bearing the same inscriptions:

" Ici est mort un soldat francais No. . . . . .
    tombé au Champ d'Honneur, 20 août, 1914."

and here a more elaborate cross, a dead
commandant, and there a cross marked,
"Ici est mort un soldat allemand." We
walked on, a silent trio. I was thinking
of a year ago, of the wives and families of
these heroes already almost forgotten.

Now we came to a little village surrounded with trees. On our left, some kilometres away, we saw the " 75's " bursting
above the Germans. Sitting down with
some soldiers who were taking shelter, we
watched for an hour these "75's" bursting, foot by foot, along the enemy's
trenches. Again we started on our way
and passed a hole cut in the road where a
German shell had burst not long since.

At last we saw Nomeny — a town of some thirteen hundred inhabitants, placed on the side of a hill and running down to the river Seille, where it ends as abruptly as it starts. Just a charming little town, harmonizing with the surrounding country as only French villages can. We made out the tower of the ninth-century church and the walls of an old ruined castle. The sun blazed on the scene and we stood there looking with true pleasure on this delightful evidence of French genius in combining architecture and scenery. The road curved to the right for some two kilometres. Here Nomeny is hidden from sight. A turn to the left and there again it stands with its old castle. But what an illusion distance had played upon our sight. Ruined castle! Why, the castle walls are the only things that are *not* ruined. There stands Nomeny's skeleton. Not a roof, not a particle of wood remains! Just the bare walls of the houses.

We arrived at the outskirts of the town
and presenting ourselves at the commandant's bureau, a lieutenant offered
to show us over the town. I cannot describe it. No words could adequately
convey the sickening sense of desolation
and desecration. Here are the facts.
The Fourth and Eighth Bavarian regiments, on August 20, decided to loot the
town. *Camions* coming from Metz took
away everything of value. Every house
was burned, house by house, men, women
and children being shot as they tried to
escape. Those who were in the basements
of the houses were shot there, or burning
petrol poured into the cellars. When the
French arrived (our guide was one of the
first arrivals), they had to bury sixty mur-
dered civilians.

Our long tramp home was uneventful,
though very tiring — except when we came
to the little village where we had rested
and lunched with the "75's" bursting

THE WRECK OF THE GERMAN AEROPLANE

some kilometres away. Here we found
two trees across the road, and on making
inquiries learned that the Germans had
seen the General's staff car going along
the road (did I explain that the whole
length of this road is in full view of the
enemy?) and seeing the car enter the wood
and not emerging on the other side, bombarded the wood, and were successful in
wounding the General's chauffeur.

Yesterday we went to Fey-en-Haye,
and we saw quite another thing. This little village, a bit larger than Montauville,
is as completely destroyed as Nomeny.
It is true that the church was dynamited
by the Germans, but here we have a legiti-
mate excuse. The village was of strate-
gical importance and the absolute destruction was done after the evacuation of the
civilians. The ruins look as different from
those of Nomeny as could be imagined.
No skeleton remains; it simply has been
destroyed by shell fire, hundreds and hun-

dreds of shells, both French and German. The whole place looks as if some great eruption had occurred and leveled it to the ground. Whether it was necessary or not, I don't know, but here one gets the feeling of war and shell, while at Nomeny it is — different.

September 29th.

Last Monday, we heard the news of the English and French victory in the Champagne. The shelling of the French trenches in the Bois-le-Prêtre had been awful all day, but when the good news spread it sent courage to all the depressed, so that within a short time, the woods rang with cheers and shouts of "à la bayonette!"

To-day, lots of nice letters came from America. The last two days have been full of excitement and we have been given an additional *secteur* to evacuate; consequently our Section has been temporarily divided in two. "Mac" and I remain in Pont-à-Mousson. An attack is expected daily and with it will come the usual heavy bombardment of Pont-à-Mousson and the main roads. At present the rain has stopped everything and the French and English successes will, I suppose, be checked, as the heavy rain will make advances almost impossible.

September 30th.

News came this morning that 40,000 prisoners had been taken by the Allies and that three army corps had passed through the lines at Champagne. It all seems too good to be true, the first great good news the brave French have had for twelve months. Rain, rain, rain, all day long; therefore, I do not expect we shall have immediate trouble here. The winter has come — the cold weather is very bad and a night call is an unpleasant business.

The other evening when returning with

an empty car, I asked a sentry whom I knew at Dieulouard (from which point onward we are allowed no light) if there was much traffic ahead. "Oh, no," he answered, "not much — it is mostly past now." So with a "good-night" I started ahead — and six feet farther on I ran straight into a horse!

October 10th.

To-day I saw one of the most exciting episodes I have seen since I came out here. Several German aviatics and French planes had been flying over the trenches and so many shots were fired by both German and French guns that there were at least a hundred white puffs of smoke against the sky. About a half an hour after, three or four shells were thrown into the town and I went up to the top floor of our house to watch them explode. A German aeroplane could be seen on our lines reconnoitering, when suddenly another plane, a Nieuport, came tearing down upon it. We gave a shout, "A Frenchman! A fight! Vive la France!" The Frenchman was now above the German, the German in full retreat. Lower and lower dropped the Frenchman, always overtaking the German. Bang! bang! bang! went the *mitrailleuses*. The German swerved — the Frenchman was level — now he was underneath! Bang! bang! bang! A yell went up from us all. The German was hit. His plane swerved, right side, left side, dipped, curved, dipped, nose to the ground, a puff of smoke — something had exploded in the machine; it was now dropping straight to the earth — and finally was lost to sight in the woods of Puvenelle. We yelled, we shrieked, we cheered, — the Frenchman had won! A dull roar came from the woods of Bois-le-Prêtre, thousands of French voices cheering the success of their comrade.

You may imagine the excitement at dinner when George Roeder and Willis, who had not been with us, marched into the room triumphant, with bits of the German aeroplane.

October 13th.

Yesterday was a serious day for us and I had a bit of an escape. You will have seen, I expect, that we were badly bombarded and that incendiary shells were thrown into the town. It was a Sunday — it is always a Sunday. "*Gott mit uns,*" I suppose!

Well, about ten o'clock I started off to pay a visit to a "wireless" friend with whom I had been learning to read. An aeroplane flew overhead and I pronounced it to be a Frenchman. I was in the middle of the road when I heard the whistle of a shell a long way off, but, strange to say, *over* my head. It came nearer and nearer, louder and louder. Have you ever actually experienced that inability to move which sometimes comes in a dream? I did then, for the first (and I hope for the only) time in my life. Louder and louder shrieked the shell and I just stood in the middle of the street paralyzed. I could not move. At last — bang! And then I ran, ran like a bolted rabbit. Of course, it was ludicrously late, but luckily for me the aeroplane bomb, for such it was, dropped twenty metres from me, *on the other side of a stone wall*. I need scarcely say I was ragged for my inability to distinguish a Frenchman from a German, but it is not so easy as one would imagine.

After lunch, Ben and I went to pay a visit to some of our friends in the trenches and afterwards walked through the first line for some time.

About three o'clock, we heard a heavy bombardment, the shells passing over our heads in the direction of the town. We walked to the edge of the hill and sitting down watched the poor little place being shelled for two hours. The explosions of the German shells and the shrieking of the French ones as they flew overhead to silence the German batteries was most impressive.

At last, one shell came very near the house where Ben and I lived and was followed shortly after by a second, even nearer. Ben jumped up exclaiming, "Come on. I can't watch that any more; it is too close to our house and I have a new winter uniform there."

We returned to our friends' dugouts about six and had an excellent supper in the open with stars and trees as a background and a gramophone to provide music, 600 metres from the Germans.

The other day, we took another walk through the woods further back from those I have been talking about, where the Germans were last September. Shell-holes everywhere, and old trenches marked the battle lines. Violets had already appeared and I picked a few and put them in my fatigue-cap. Passing along a little wood-path, we came upon the inevitable harvest, — two wooden crosses, side by side — but different! One cross was more carefully hewn, and nailed to it by a bullet was a little piece of red cloth, the color of the trousers the French infantry wore at the beginning of the war, and which is said to have cost France several hundred thousand men. The other cross was just two sticks, and hanging on it was a piece of gray-blue, — a German. So here, side by side, a long, long way from town or village, in the silence of the wood, lie two nameless soldiers. Foes? I wonder.

. . . .

So the days pass — Now, with the evening, comes, as often, a grateful time of stillness. I like to watch from my window the shadows lengthen as the sun leaves to them their part. A little later, when they have wholly obscured all detail, man will perhaps furtively begin some move to make the night unlovely — but for the moment there is rest.

An owl has just hooted — a musty old clock has just struck six — a convoy wagon rumbling along the road raises a cloud of golden dust — then silence again.

Lately I have discovered a beautiful garden full of fruit and flowers where an old man still stays as caretaker. Schroeder and I go there often and eat the fruit which is spoiling on the trees.

Sometimes — when the day's work is done — and there is a quiet hour here, it is good to think of other gardens far away where the salt air comes in from the sea — or often the fog, on these still summer evenings. I can understand now the lure of peace — and so I am doubly grateful that those of you for whom I care most have chosen to work — rather than to forget the struggle here. When I come back to you some day, we shall feel a greater peace and sympathy for knowing that with the same eagerness, if in different ways, we have tried to serve and to save those men whose heroism makes our best effort seem a very small thing.

THE END

www.ingramcontent.com/pod-product-compliance
Lightning Source LLC
Chambersburg PA
CBHW030826090426
42737CB00009B/898